Praise for
The Dance of Defiance

"I find it so inspirational to see a parent who has actually 'walked the walk' or, in this situation 'danced the dance,' speak about parenting and the needs of children. Nancy's book is refreshing and enlightening on so many levels and from a variety of perspectives. Her book provides a road map for other parents on the same hazardous journey of trying to navigate a less-than-family-friendly system to get services to help their child."

Steven R. Isham
Child & Family Advocate/Educator

"A beacon of light for those in need, a document of research for those exploring, and a deep heartfelt story, this book has just the right ingredients for all. In this book, written firsthand by a parent who has experienced heartache and overcome obstacles, you can feel the dedication and emotion. A book genuinely written for the sole purpose of making information accessible, it conveys all the important aspects of raising a child with oppositional defiant disorder, including strategies, and a motivational story of hope. Written by a parent for other parents, this book is not one to be passed up."

Abby Hagener
Recreation Leader/Daughter

"Life is not always what you plan for it to be. And who can escape life's 'trial by fire' to see if you 'turn out gold'? This family's journey gives us a glimpse of such a trial. It takes us from fear and heartache to a place of hope. 'Bumps in the road' are smoothed out with a loving mother's perseverance, faith, and instinct as she learns to be thankful for and to savor precious moments. Heartwarming and inspiring, *The Dance of Defiance* gives hope to the seemingly hopeless task of caring for an intelligent, serious, sensitive, yet oftentimes difficult, child. Satan knows where to hurt us most deeply, but God knows how to turn it into something good for those who let Him."

Jimmie Lou Watson
Education Specialist/Author

"A support group in a book! Nancy Hagener has allowed us to journey with her into the real struggle of parenting a child with ODD. Despite the struggle, she never lost hope. And that, to many families experiencing hardship, is the most empowering gift of all. This book is not only valuable to families but to professionals as we strive to understand and empathize with families who deal with possibly the most misunderstood child - one with ODD. I am amazed at Nancy's courage to let others in and give voice to her family's experience. I have no doubt that countless families will be blessed as a result."

Kathleen Richardson
BSW, MSW Candidate, University of Michigan

"The burden is impossible to carry alone; shame creates a barrier to sharing; Nancy Hagener has embraced a responsibility and turned it into an opportunity for insight and knowledge in uncharted waters. In so doing she has communicated a legacy of correct understanding into the psyches of children so misunderstood that they are driven into further depths of angry despair and alienation. We can now say—no more!"

Jill G. Jones-Soderman,
Psychoanalyst/Family Therapist

The
Dance
of
Defiance

A Mother and Son Journey with
Oppositional Defiant Disorder

Nancy A. Hagener, MAEd.

With a Foreword by Louis G. Trunzo, M.D.

Shamrock
Books, LLC

Requests for such permission should be addressed to:
Shamrock Books
11445 E. Via Linda, Ste. 2
PMB 321
Scottsdale, AZ 85259
www.shamrockbooks.com

Welcome to Holland
© 1987 by Emily Perl Kingsley, used with permission

Unless noted, all scripture notations are taken from the *Life Application Study Bible*, New International Version (NIV). Copyright 1973, 1978, 1984 by International Bible Society.

The names of individuals in "Shared Stories" have been changed to protect their privacy.

Hagener, Nancy A.
The Dance of Defiance:
A Mother and Son Journey With Oppositional Defiant Disorder

Cover Design: Manjari Graphics
Layout: J. L. Saloff
Fonts used: Goudy, Papyrus

Hardbound ISBN: 0-9765579-0-8
Perfectbound ISBN: 0-9765579-1-6
Library of Congress Control Number: 2005923753
Copyright information available upon request.

First Edition
Printed on acid free paper in The United States of America

To My Family

Ian Patrick
With whom I've learned how deeply the human heart can love.
Through despair and challenges, we still danced.
It's both an honor and a privilege to call you my son.

Abby
Whose gentle spirit and kind heart made her the peacemaker.
You never gave up, never lost faith, and always loved.
I thank God each day for the joy of you, sweet daughter.

Roger
My husband who was always there.
Like the sailor that you are, you never left the helm.

Difficult times have helped me to understand better than before, how infinitely rich and beautiful life is in every way, and that so many things that one goes worrying about are of no importance whatsoever.

Isak Dinesen

Welcome to Holland

By Emily Perl Kingsley

I am often asked to describe the experience of raising a child with a disability - to try to help people who have not shared that unique experience to understand it, to imagine how it would feel. It's like this......

When you're going to have a baby, it's like planning a fabulous vacation trip - to Italy. You buy a bunch of guide books and make your wonderful plans. The Coliseum. The Michelangelo David. The gondolas in Venice. You may learn some handy phrases in Italian. It's all very exciting.

After months of eager anticipation, the day finally arrives. You pack your bags and off you go. Several hours later, the plane lands. The stewardess comes in and says, "Welcome to Holland."

"Holland?!?" you say. "What do you mean Holland?? I signed up for Italy! I'm supposed to be in Italy. All my life I've dreamed of going to Italy."

But there's been a change in the flight plan. They've landed in Holland and there you must stay.

The important thing is that they haven't taken you to a horrible, disgusting, filthy place, full of pestilence, famine and disease. It's just a different place.

So you must go out and buy new guide books. And you must learn a whole new language. And you will meet a whole new group of people you would never have met.

It's just a different place. It's slower-paced than Italy, less flashy than Italy. But after you've been there for a while and you catch your breath, you look around…. and you begin to notice that Holland has windmills…. and Holland has tulips. Holland even has Rembrandts.

But everyone you know is busy coming and going from Italy… and they're all bragging about what a wonderful time they had there. And for the rest of your life, you will say "Yes, that's where I was supposed to go. That's what I had planned."

And the pain of that will never, ever, ever, ever go away… because the loss of that dream is a very significant loss.

But… if you spend your life mourning the fact that you didn't get to Italy, you may never be free to enjoy the very special, the very lovely things… about Holland.

Table of Contents

Foreword

Babies conjure thoughts of future presidents, ballerinas, and baseball stars. No one plans to conceive a challenging child! Without the knowledge of the road ahead, Nancy conceived her baby with all those hopes and dreams. From her newborn boy's first cry, the challenges began. Nancy knew there was something different about this child compared to her first. This would be a challenging child!

This book, written by a parent for parents, sends a powerful message of hope for the parents of challenging children. Nancy's journey with her son is explored in depth in *The Dance of Defiance*. Nancy's story is not unlike those of many other families I have cared for in my pediatric practice. In a marvelous way she embraces her responsibility and shares from her heart. Her spirituality shines through as she shares the difficulties her family endured while rearing a challenging child. As the journey unfolds, pearls of wisdom are revealed to the reader who may be in a family in crisis. This book will serve as a guide and a resource for families facing these same or similar challenges.

Challenging children and adolescents can cause disharmony within families. Nancy intimately shares her shame and her isolation from friends and family. Nancy tried to keep up a front that she had the "perfect family." This only led to greater disharmony and despair.

Nancy's realization that she needed to reach out to family, friends, colleagues, and professionals and share her anguish was the beginning of healing for her family. This healing led to greater understanding and open-mindedness about treatment options for her son. Positive solutions evolve from understanding there is no one answer. In fact, it takes a team of individuals to break through these burdens. It is impossible to carry these burdens alone.

She further details that the team for success will include not only loved ones and friends but also a psychotherapist, a pediatrician, and teachers, to name a few of the caring, intelligent individuals who can listen, guide, suggest, and support the family with compassion. All reasonable modalities should be explored, including medication. This is a big step for most, and Nancy shares her difficulty in the book. Nancy exhausted all possibilities before seriously considering medication. I suggest that each child has a unique biology, and therapies and medications need to be tailored to each special individual.

Nancy shares her insights in the hope that each child can have the opportunity to have a healthy mind. The journey is a process, as is life. This process is continuous and routinely requires attention. Children grow and develop, which implies change. This change may consequently require reestablishing therapy or changing doses and medications. Many children and adolescents suffer from more than one diagnosis. This is also known as having comorbid conditions. As the journey unfolds, new opportunities evolve with new research and new medications.

The Dance of Defiance is a gift to all those on a similar journey. A spirit of hope and a framework from which to build a support team around your family await you in the pages that follow. What are you waiting for?

Louis G. Trunzo, MD, FAAP
Medical Director
North Valley Pediatrics

Preface

I've heard people comment that they "knew something was different from the beginning," when describing their special child. My son, Ian, came into the world red-faced, wailing, and hungry. To say he was "demanding" would be an understatement. He just had an urgency about him and it was obvious to all around him. This sense of urgency quickly permeated our household. The goal was to have him calm, well-fed, and happy. The reality was oftentimes different.

We managed to take care of the day-to-day necessities and enjoyed the good moments. They were too few. I was becoming aware of a growing fear in the pit of my stomach. As Ian got older, his temper got bigger. By the time he was two, my daughter, Abby, was already making herself scarce when his temper tantrums would begin. He was putting words to his demands and it was not pleasant. This was more than the "terrible twos." My little son was angry! I mean, really angry!

We rode this roller coaster until he was three. By that time I was telling the pediatrician, "Something is not right." At which he explained that my son was a typically active and healthy boy. The doctor went on to point out that Ian had a different personality than Abby and smiled as he tried to reassure me. No, there was more. During this visit, I explained to the doctor that I wondered if Ian's lead levels were elevated after we had done some remodeling on our fifty-year-old home. Did the construction stir up some lead from old paint? Had this caused the behavior problem? I asked to have Ian's blood tested for lead poisoning. The results were negative. Absolutely normal.

I thought, "This must be behavioral." Discipline tactics which had worked with my daughter were laughed at by my son. Time out in a chair? No way. He would defiantly get up from that chair and walk away. There was no way I could physically keep him in a time-out. A spanking? He seemed to enjoy the challenge. This simply brought us down to his level and engaged us in a no-win power struggle. We certainly weren't going to beat him into compliancy.

So what were we to do? I was a mom at a complete loss, beginning to feel the weight of raising a challenging child. I realized that my parenting skills, while successful with my daughter, weren't going to be enough for Ian. As if preparing for battle, I had to read, ask questions, search for answers, and build myself up. It wasn't going to be easy; the best things in life rarely are. But the results were certainly worth it.

N.A.H.

Acknowledgments

We did not travel alone on our journey; many special individuals accompanied us along the way. Their support and encouragement helped make this book a reality. My heartfelt thank you to the following individuals:

Kathy Richardson, Judy Norton, Patty Sayed, and John Lazzeri, my sisters and brother. Growing up the youngest of five children, I was affectionately referred to as the "caboose." I am grateful to have been on that train. Thanks for teaching me all about sibling love.

John and Phyllis Lazzeri, my parents. In our home, we lived secure in the knowledge of having a mother who loved unconditionally, laughed uncontrollably, and sang beautifully. Mom, a.k.a. Pilby, you modeled what a mother's love is. I continue to watch as you live out that example of love and dedication. Dad, a.k.a. Giovanni, you are a man of integrity, who passed on his love of languages and rich family heritage. I continue to look to you for inspiration as you live your life with courage, determination, and faith. Thank you, Mom and Dad, your legacy of love continues in each of us.

John and Kathy Richardson, my brother-in-law and sister to whom I looked for wisdom and insight throughout the writing of this book. Day or night, by phone, email and instant messaging sessions, you were always there for me. Your support, love, and presence in my life are a great blessing.

Dr. Gene Carsia, Dr. Drake D. Duane, Dr. Roger M. Martig, Dr. Marilyn Millman, Dr. Natalie Schoenbauer, Jill G. Jones-Soderman,

Dr. Louis G. Trunzo, and Dr. Susan Youngs, the dedicated, caring professionals who gave me their support, time, and encouragement.

Steven Isham and Mary Kramer, University of Phoenix instructors who taught with wisdom and compassion and shared the vision for this book.

Susan Dankberg, a teacher who truly made a difference. Your open heart and guidance pointed us in the right direction. You have touched many lives in such a positive way during your teaching career. How thankful we are.

Prayer Warriors in Arizona and Michigan and Desert Mountain High School Moms-In-Touch members Diane McGinty, Jayne O'Connell, Barb Siko, and Irene Hausmann. Your prayers and encouraging words lifted my spirit and brought blessings throughout the writing of this book. I am honored by your prayers and thankful for your friendship.

Jimmie Lou Watson, my dear friend, fellow teacher and author, and coffee partner. Our friendship was a direct answer to prayer. You have made such a difference in my life.

Tom Bird, author and writing mentor. Your seminar started it all and, with your guidance, the idea has come to fruition.

Jamie Saloff, of Saloff Enterprises, book designer. From the start, your support, professionalism, and enthusiasm made things go smoothly.

Manjari Henderson, graphic artist. You took the vision in my mind and created it in a beautiful cover. Your talent and creativity made it such fun.

Beth Phillips, Eagle Eye Editor. Not only did you edit the work, you taught me the process of clear, concise writing as we progressed. Learning about your Scottish heritage, when we first met in your home amongst beautiful heather, Scottish books, and Scottish artwork, was an added bonus.

Roger, Abby, and Ian, my family. Roger, thank you for giving me the precious gift of time to write. Your endless patience, encouragement, and love never wavered. Abby, I loved our late night conversations and your encouraging words. You always found me right where you left me—at the computer. Ian, by sharing our story, we may reach others with the gift of hope and help change lives. That's really what it's all about. Thank you, son, for letting us share this incredible journey. You put the music in my heart and the musical notes on the cover!

God. All along, I believed this book was being written by the Holy Spirit. I was only the instrument. It was His gentle nudging that started it and His incredible blessings that made it a reality.

Introduction

I saw the scene unfolding as I pulled into my parking space. At the time, I was employed as an instructional assistant in special education at a local elementary school. A woman was in the process of trying to drop her son off for a day at school. Her car pulled up to the curb in the drop-off lane and her son jumped out. The first bell had already rung, and the playground and sidewalks were deserted. First I heard the voice. You may know that voice: one of frustration bordering on rage. As I glanced over, I could feel myself in her skin. You may know that feeling of being pulled into a place where reason and rationality do not exist. Of wanting so badly to be anywhere but where you are at that very moment. The feeling of utter helplessness and inability to control the events. Your heart starts to beat faster and your shoulders tense. You are breathing faster and your hands begin to sweat. You're going into what's known as "fight or flight" mode, survival tactics as you deal with this child.

You are in a world separate from the other parents who drop off their children every day with few or no problems at all. This woman, on that early morning, was in that separate world. The first thing I saw was the woman standing face to face with the boy, holding onto both of his arms as he pulled with all his might to break free from her grip. He was a pretty good-sized boy and looked almost stronger than she. Depending on how long this behavior had been going on, the woman's physical and emotional strength had likely been diminishing by the day.

She let go as he yelled and moved over to the trunk of the car, which he slammed hard with his hand. She told him firmly, "Pick up your backpack." To which he replied, "No, I'm already late! The first bell rang!" Pure anger and rage at this woman, who looked so tired and defeated. Rage from a boy that couldn't be older than ten.

If you've lived this scene, or one similar to it, you know as well as I do that the young boy would not be picking his backpack up anytime soon. Defiance. His mother bent down, picked it up, and put it over one of his shoulders. She then turned him toward the school, muttered good-bye, and got back into her car. Without looking back, she drove off to face the rest of her day, leaving an angry, hostile boy at the curb all before 8:30 in the morning. The tone had been set for the day. The mom and son were locked in the grip of defiance, yet life went on. They each had responsibilities: job, school, and relationships. Unfortunately, they would both carry that burden of stress with them throughout their day.

I purposely walked past that scene, not to be nosy but quite possibly to rescue her. I wanted to help her and say, "It is okay. I know what you are living. Feel the compassion I have in my heart for you. You will not be judged by me as being a bad parent. I won't judge how tired you look, what kind of car you drive, how your son is dressed, and more important, how he is acting toward you. It is not your fault. He needs help. You need intervention and rescuing. This will not get better. It will only get worse. Before it destroys the life of your child, it will most likely destroy your life, your marriage, and your family."

As I passed, instead of speaking to her I spoke a silent prayer for her and for her son as well, who most likely does not like living with rage and anger the way he does. It is a slippery slope we're on in these situations, one in which there are few clear paths and directions to take when we realize we have a problem. It is isolating, depressing, and destroying.

Our path to healing lasted about eight years. Throughout that time I was searching for answers and feeling more and more consumed by our circumstances. Being a voracious reader, I went to the library and searched for everything I could find on raising difficult children. Once we actually had a diagnosis, my search narrowed to anything on oppositional defiant disorder (ODD). I found plenty on attention deficit disorder (ADD), autism, Down syndrome, and learning disabilities. Within those books, upon searching the index I would sometimes discover a one-paragraph blip addressing ODD. The mention was vague and didn't give me anything more than I already knew. Most books on the shelves were written by doctors. While these were excellent references, I was looking for a book written from a parent's perspective by someone who had lived it. I needed a book written by a parent for parents.

I've always had a love for words and writing. In the back of my mind I thought sometime in the future I would write that book I had been searching for. During the storm of our lives, however, I wasn't thinking of writing about it. Any and all energy I had was used in caring for my son and my family. Most evenings, I had no desire to write and reflect upon all that had taken place that day. My only desire was to sleep and escape the turmoil although I did keep excellent records and I'm thankful for that. I believe, finally, that we've found some direction, and, most important, hope for the future. After some time and healing I'm able to share our story. In doing so, I hope to encourage, support, and affirm you in caring for your challenging child.

If you've found yourself saying, "I've been there. That's me. That's my son/daughter," then this book may be a beacon of light and hope for you. If given a choice, I wouldn't have chosen a son with these special needs. I'm now able to realize that I was blessed with this son. Did I say blessed? Yes! Because of Ian, I have learned countless lessons in life, love, patience, and forgiveness. Most of all, I've discovered true compassion. The kind of compassion you feel physically because you have lived it. The lessons continue each and every day. They are carried into words of kindness to a tired store clerk, to a mom in the grocery store with three young children, to my students and to my own family.

While I didn't set out to write this book with a Christian perspective, if I left out the spiritual part of the journey, this book would be profoundly incomplete. Leaving out those essential details would be cheating you out of a very precious gift. You don't have to share my faith; you can gain insight from this book no matter what your beliefs or background may be.

I believe this journey was all part of a master plan. All this didn't happen by chance; there had to be a reason for it. I firmly believe that God was shaping me through these experiences to grow my faith, to learn to depend on Him, and to share with others what I've discovered in raising a challenging child. God used me for the purpose of comforting and strengthening others through my story of hope. He's using me now to reach out to you.

Along with love and discipline, my parents raised me with the gift of faith. It was that foundation of faith I relied on; through the trials and tribulations, it was the one thing that never wavered. It was when I completely surrendered to God and truly began a personal relationship with Him that I understood how much He loved me. All those lonely times? He was with me. Holding on fiercely to my son, our bodies wracked with violent sobs? God was holding me. Being bitten, spat on, and cursed? He was there, holding my hand. Sitting alone in an empty house, crying silently? He shed tears with me.

Throughout this journey, I had been looking for help from my husband, doctors, and therapists. I thought if I could just find the right person to help my son, everything would work out. He was there all along. I was about to discover that.

One night, after an especially hard day, I found myself where I needed to be all along: on my knees. As I knelt, exhausted and weary at the side of Ian's bed, I wept and surrendered to God. I could not do this alone. I couldn't even do it with the best professional help. I needed to turn it over to God, lift my son to Him, and believe in His Word that says, "The Lord is close to the brokenhearted and saves those who are crushed in spirit" Psalm 34:18. I discovered that in reaching the end of myself, I was able to reach Christ. I was at the end; He was waiting for me.

Since that night, I have been on my knees while my son sleeps. Sometimes he wakes and through barely opened eyes, smiles at me.

He knows his mom is praying for him and loving him. Better yet, I know God is loving both of us.

To be honest, there are days I wish I hadn't been blessed in this unique way. Days in which I didn't feel on guard for possible meltdowns. Days that didn't include walking on eggs. But the very same days that took me to despair also took me to a place of discovery. I will continue to learn these and more lessons as they unfold, throughout my son's unique and challenging journey in life.

Through this book, I would like to share what I have learned in our journey. My goal is to hold out hope for those of us who are in that separate, isolated world where our children are challenged and we are desperate for help and hope. A world where physical disabilities elicit compassion while behavioral, chemical, or biological imbalances elicit harsh judgment and unfounded criticism. We need the same compassion our society shows toward physical challenges. We are the caregivers and advocates for our children. We need support, encouragement, and respite from the daily energy we pour into their care. Throughout our journey, I have discovered there is hope and there is help. I pray that this book is the first step in your journey toward peace, in knowing that you are not alone, and in discovering the blessing that is your special child.

1

Beyond the Pediatrician

After bringing my son home from the hospital, I quickly learned what the term "colicky" meant and how blessed I was that I hadn't experienced it with my daughter. Doctors aren't sure what causes colic, but they define it generally as continued crying for three or more hours a day. This crying is not caused by wet diapers or hunger, and it cannot be stopped by usual calming methods. Some doctors believe that colic is simply a baby's temperament as he or she adjusts to the world, food, and sleep cycles. The good news is that colic usually stops after three months.

Both breastfed and bottle-fed babies may experience colic. In our case, my attempts at breastfeeding were not successful. We then discovered that Ian was allergic to milk, leading us to try soy-based formulas. This is when you discover what your pediatrician and his or her staff are really made of. Experienced nurses gave me endless support and encouragement over the phone as my son wailed in the background. They suggested (and we tried) the following:

- *Put the baby across my lap, on his stomach, and rub his back*
- *Burp the baby more often during feeding*
- *Walk with the baby*
- *Rock the baby in a rocking chair*
- *Put the baby in his car seat and take him for a soothing drive*

- *Put the baby in a swing to experience the soothing
  rocking motion*

It was this last suggestion that really saved us—the swing. You quickly run through all the suggested strategies and find out what works. Ian spent a great deal of time, lulled to sleep in the comfort of the swing.

The days and nights that followed were really a blur. Looking back, I believe Ian's colic was a combination of his temperament and his sensitivity to milk products. I do recall the symptoms letting up after a few months. Those of you who have survived raising a colicky baby can relate to the way time seems to stand still and the days all run together. We've all heard stories of parents driving their babies around the neighborhood to calm them down.

Caring for a colicky baby can be exhausting and draining. It's important to follow-up with a pediatrician to be sure there are no other causes for the baby's distress. It is equally important to take care of yourself and the rest of your family. Enlist the help of families, neighbors, and friends to give you a little relief throughout the colicky days. It also helps to remind yourself that colic usually ends by about three months of age.

Asking Questions

We've all been told somewhere along the way to always "get a second opinion" when given a diagnosis or treatment plan. Everyone would agree that's common sense. However, as parents struggling with special children we need to take that advice one step further. We need to realize that different professionals view emotional and behavioral disorders in various ways. Their educational background, training, experience, and philosophy on children will affect their methods of treatment. As parents desperate to find help for our child, we often meet these professionals when we're exhausted. We are experiencing a myriad of emotions: fatigue, anger, fear, and anxiety. We aren't always approaching that first meeting armed with background questions although we should be. I was about to learn first-hand how important it is to make sure I know where that professional stands on methods and treatment.

We had the kind of pediatrician young moms fall in love with. Well, maybe not literally, but they did notice his striking good looks, not to mention the French accent. Yes, he was educated in France. What woman wouldn't find that attractive? Me, I didn't care what the man looked like; I was so tired I hardly noticed anyway. All I wanted was some direction for my son. Could he help me figure out how to help Ian? I would explain the difficulties we were experiencing. After a physical exam, he would tell me that Ian was strong-willed and would likely grow up to be a strong leader. He would do great things. As wonderful as that sounded, I wasn't interested in what kind of an adult he would become. I was interested in the here and now. I needed help with raising him and I needed that help immediately. Looking back, this was the start of my asking doctors for help, desperately at times, and not getting any real, immediate, concrete solutions. When we visited their offices, they never saw the true defiance we were facing. I felt like I couldn't make anyone understand the reality we were living.

I was dealing with a child who was constantly frustrated by simple things. When playing, he would try to fit several things into a toy bus, for example, and they did not fit. I would see his frustration building and try to distract him with something else. It would not work. Once he was on that slippery slope, there was no stopping him. He would become enraged, yelling, screaming, and throwing the toy.

I would take Ian to visit my parents, his grandparents. It was too seldom a fun experience. Several times the following scenario unfolded upon our arrival: we would pull into their driveway, and I would open the door to get Ian from his car seat. He would decide he did not want to go in. This was a problem, especially during the winter season in the Midwest. I would try to remain calm, and even cheerful, when he stiffened up as I unbuckled him. When we entered the house, he would start arching his back and screaming. He was so angry that I took him in, he was throwing a tantrum. It got to the point that upon entering my parents' home, I would turn around, take my kicking, screaming son right back to the car, and go back home. Looking back, I'm sure this behavior baffled my parents, who had raised five kids with no serious discipline problems. I still have visions of Mom's and Dad's uncomfortable and bewildered expressions as we abruptly left their home.

Leaving my parents' house seemed like a good solution since by then Ian was in a rage and I was discouraged and upset. However, getting him back into the car seat was another problem. He would arch his back and stiffen again, to the point I could not get him buckled into that seat! I'm sure it was quite a sight from my mom's window.

Ian was almost three now, and finally, I insisted that the pediatrician refer us to a family therapist. We had explored medical problems and all seemed to be normal. I thought it had to be behavioral. We were referred to a doctor who specialized in individual and family therapy. He was a PhD on staff at our hospital and well-respected by our pediatrician. We made the appointment and started what was the beginning of our journey with therapy. This also marked the beginning of learning the true meaning of isolation.

Controversial Therapy

In our desperate attempt to help our son, we began therapy once a week. We didn't do our homework. We went into the initial consultation looking for a solution to years of struggles. We hadn't done this before; there was no handbook for us to use. We didn't know what questions to ask. Instead, we met this doctor, viewed his various educational degrees displayed in his office, and put our trust in him.

This doctor had worked with troubled kids ranging in age from as young as our son to the teens; we were hopeful he could help Ian. He shared success stories of working with children and teens to help them regain control of themselves through a holding method. This is where the controversial part of the therapy comes in. The doctor explained that we needed to show Ian that we were in charge and that he would be okay, that he was safe.

The doctor went on to explain that, when the child went into a rage, we needed to hold him until he calmed down. In order to do this with a child in a full-blown rage, I had to sit on the floor, with my legs folded, with Ian also on the floor, his back to me. I would need to cross my arms and legs over him, holding him as he screamed and raged. All the while, it was imperative that we stay calm, and say things like "It's okay. I'm in charge. Get control." My husband and I exchanged glances which said, "I'm not so sure about this." Yet we continued to listen. We were desperate.

This would go on until he surrendered. When the child relaxed and gave in, spent and exhausted, it was over. The theory was that he would learn we are the parents. The therapist advised us to keep a log of every single tantrum in which we held Ian. Note the time, duration, and any important details. The goal was to be able to return to normal discipline methods as soon as possible once we changed the behavior. Once Ian knew we were the parents, we were in charge.

Now, mind you, all this had to take place whenever he went into a tantrum. If the doorbell was ringing, we were to ignore it. If the phone rang, ignore it. If we had company over, take him to another room and close the door. If I was on my way to an appointment, cancel it. Everything had to take second place to holding Ian when he was in a rage. This was where the incredible isolation in my life began.

Seven Secluded Months

Every family has its own dynamics. In our family, I tended to be the disciplinarian. Hence, when it came time to hold Ian through tantrums, I was the one who most consistently did it. Being home with my children, I was also the one present most of the time. So I was the one who held Ian. Almost daily for seven months. First, I carefully noted the date and time of each occurrence. Next, I wrote down what I believed triggered the episode, anything from frustration over a missing puzzle piece to wanting to play in the rain (during thunder and lightning). Finally, I noted the duration of the holding and what took place. Looking back at my handwritten log, it all comes back to me. During these times, Ian would become so enraged he would spit at me, and once he even bit my wrist. He would scream that he had to go to the bathroom, that he hated me, and that I was stupid. Had he known any swear words, I am convinced these would have been spewed at me as well. These were violent, sweaty, teary episodes that would last, on average, thirty minutes. The most violent one, when Ian bit me, lasted a full fifty minutes. I would pray and tears would silently fall. I began to see it as a spiritual battle. It was a very frightening situation. The episodes would end with Ian crying and falling asleep. By this time, we were both physically and emotionally exhausted. Imagine a mother and son, sitting on the floor, against a wall, soaked with sweat, tears, and spit while the son, exhausted, sleeps in her arms. Imagine the fear the mother felt.

This happened almost every day. In some cases, more than once a day. It happened enough to cause our family to become really dysfunctional. I quit answering the phone. Oftentimes, I didn't answer the door. I imagine the nearby neighbors heard the screaming and wondered what was going on. My daughter could not have friends over for fear that her brother would go into a rage. She also became more distant as she suffered through listening to these rages.

I became resentful of my husband's getting dressed and going off to work each day. He could have conversations with rational adults. He could go to motivational sales seminars. He could go out to lunch. I was at home for these seven months, alone with Ian, in distress, and completely isolated from family and friends. I didn't meet friends, have a break, or recharge myself in any way. I had not let anyone in at this point and was trying to keep up the appearance of a happy family.

We knew we were in serious trouble. This approach clearly was not working. In fact, it was beginning to seriously depress me, put a wedge in our marriage, and isolate our daughter. Ian was seriously troubled. This therapy was not helping him. After several phone calls to the doctor and seven months of weekly visits, we stopped the treatment. There had to be a better solution.

Looking back on this awful time, I realize how very desperate we were. Anyone who lived through days like we had can relate to that desperation. I learned from this experience to trust my instincts over that of a professional when I have that persistent feeling that things aren't right. Call it "mother's instinct" or a "gut feeling." When it comes to raising our children, we are the experts. Our mother's instinct or gut feelings are usually right. It is easier for me to say that, now that we've come so far from that terrible time.

Nancy A. Hagener

2

Wide Open Spaces

It's funny how life does continue, even in a severely stressed family. Roger had an offer to take an early buyout from his business. It was a "once-in-a-lifetime opportunity" we knew wouldn't come along again. We considered this offer and what it could mean for our family. We felt a relocation would be less traumatic for Abby and Ian, at ages eleven and four respectively, than when they were in junior high or high school. The timing seemed right.

Being the youngest of five siblings, I was struggling for autonomy. I remember intense feelings of never being taken seriously. Even married with two children, I felt this need to carve out my own identity. I viewed this life change as my chance to become my own person. In my search for independence, I hadn't let my siblings in to help with Ian. I had shut them out as well, in keeping with my "perfect family" image. I would later learn how great a mistake I was making by doing that. I just couldn't see it yet.

Earlier in our marriage we had talked of moving out west to a warmer climate and new opportunities. This could be a chance for a fresh start; maybe things with our family would be better. After seriously considering the offer and what it would mean to our family, we made the decision to make the move across the country to Arizona. Like so many others who have gone before us we were heading out west to discover new opportunities and a new start.

We had traveled there several times with Abby to visit grandparents, and we were somewhat familiar with the area. She was excited about the move and it seemed to be a good decision. It was an exciting yet apprehensive time. At this point, we were not in therapy. We were taking a break from it, trying to hold on each day and hope for an improvement with time. I was seeking independence, adventure, and a fresh start with my family. I was packing up our belongings, our children, and our troubles and taking them 2,000 miles away.

New Pediatrician, New Outlook

Anyone who has relocated to another state realizes the often overwhelming task of finding everything from a new grocery store to a new pediatrician. I learned to put things into order of importance. The dentist, eye doctor, and accountant could wait. Our priority was finding a good pediatrician. After the experiences of the past four years, I hoped this new beginning would bring new help for Ian. Knowing a referral is the best way to find a good doctor, I asked a young mom in my new neighborhood if she could give me the name of a good pediatrician. She said her children had a great doctor and gave me his name and number. I made the call that afternoon, to set up our first appointment.

The following week we met with Dr. Louis Trunzo, Medical Director of North Valley Pediatrics. Upon meeting him, I felt a sense of relief in his presence. He was a kind man who shared his personal background with us. He was not only the medical director of a thriving practice, he was a husband and the father of six children. He acknowledged that through the years he has experienced his share of challenges in raising a family too. It was this personal experience that gave Dr. Trunzo true insight and compassion for weary parents like us. Not only is he a respected pediatrician with twenty years in practice, he has experienced first hand the challenges of raising children. This man was real. I knew we were in the right place.

We gave him a detailed account of our family history and Ian's four-year-old medical history. He took a great deal of time giving Ian a thorough physical examination, talking with him all the while. After some questions about school, sports, and friends, Dr. Trunzo asked Ian some rather pointed questions. He took a no-nonsense approach, asking, "Why do you treat your parents this way? Why do you talk to them that way?" Ian was intimidated and I was glad! In the past, Ian would laugh in our faces as we tried to cope with his behavior. Here was Dr. Trunzo, who must have seemed like a giant to my son. He had a presence and commanded respect. Yet I could see in his eyes the compassion and love he had for people.

Dr. Trunzo's physical examination of Ian found nothing unusual. Although there are no laboratory tests, neurological assessments, or attention assessments to confirm that a person has attention deficit disorder (ADD) or attention deficit hyperactivity disorder (ADHD), he said that Ian showed signs of having one or the other. Dr. Trunzo had experience treating children with ADD and ADHD, and he had had success using medication. This was the first time we had discussed medications with a pediatrician. Although Ian had not been diagnosed with either of these disorders, they could not be ruled out yet.

Dr. Trunzo offered to try this approach to see if it would help Ian and, in the meantime, help defuse the volatile home situation we were locked in. Dr. Trunzo was the first professional to really see the trouble we were in as a family unit. He knew we were in extreme distress. By helping Ian to get control of his anger, we could then begin to get help with modifying that behavior. However, like many parents, we resisted medication and wanted to rule out any other possible treatment. Although we had tried therapy, with disastrous results, we held out hope that there was still a successful path for us. He understood this and recommended a family therapist for us to see.

Sensing our hesitation, Dr. Trunzo went on to tell us that this doctor was wonderful in working with children and families in situations just like ours. He knew the therapist personally, and we were willing to give him a try. I knew what methods we would not be open to using.

In one of our early visits with Dr. Trunzo, he actually looked at me and asked, "How are you holding up? Are you taking care of yourself through all this? Do you have support? Friends? Someone to talk to?" It was the first time a doctor stopped and took the time to sincerely ask about my physical and mental health. I found myself caught off guard.

Over the years, I had done an excellent job of keeping up the image that everything was going well in our lives. Why would anyone stop to ask how I was really doing? From all outward appearances, ours was the perfect family. How many perfect families are out there right now?

So here I was, being affirmed for the first time in how very challenging my life had been. I had found myself in so many doctors' offices in the last four years! This was the first time a doctor showed he truly cared, was empathetic, and listened to me. What a blessing he was then and continues to be.

Dr. Trunzo listened to the fact that we had recently relocated across the country, and I didn't have a support system in our new state. Because of my intense need for privacy, I hadn't had a support system in my hometown either. Not even within my own family. I had shut them out. The weight of it all was beginning to show on me. He listened and he understood. That was exactly what I needed.

We left his office that day with the name of a therapist and a feeling of having someone on our side. It would be the beginning of a valued relationship with a doctor who did indeed have love and compassion for children and families.

Six years later I found myself visiting with Dr. Trunzo as I conducted research for this book. We shared conversation and opinions on today's busy families. His compassion for children had only increased through the past few years. I learned that he now dedicates one morning a week to treating children with developmental disorders such ADD, ADHD, and ODD. We discussed how important it is that, as parents, we have a team approach to helping our children. From family doctors to pediatricians, from therapists to teachers, we need to have a good team. The ability to have this team, however, depends on the financial resources of the parents. It depends on the emotional state of the parents as well. These topics took our conversation in a new direction.

Fortunately, Roger and I had the resources to find the right help for Ian. Even though it took many years and a great deal of expense, we finally found the right combination to help Ian. What happens when parents don't have these resources? In these cases, Dr. Trunzo describes himself as "a clinician who analyzes the child and the family situation, sizes up the big picture, listens to the pain and agony, and decides what he can do to help these families whether or not they have the resources."

Parental reactions and emotions have a great impact on the child's treatment. The late well-known author, Elisabeth Kubler-Ross, described five stages of the grieving process: denial, anger, bargaining, depression, and acceptance. In raising a child with disorders like oppositional defiant disorder or attention deficit hyperactivity disorder, parents are oftentimes stuck in denial. They believe that with the right diet, behavior modification plan, or parenting skills, their child will stop the challenging behaviors. They have a hard time admitting their child needs help.

Dr. Trunzo sees parents in denial and understands that it's hard to "get someone who is experiencing denial to go from zero to sixty on the issues at hand." He went on to say, "Physicians need that special touch when working with these families to avoid alienating them. We need to be open to a variety of approaches including naturopathic therapy. We also need to remain flexible and know that medications are not the only answer to successful treatment." As parents, we need to accept our children for the unique individuals they are. While it's normal to experience denial, along with the other stages of the grieving process, we must move forward to give our children the tools they need to grow into their full potential. We are their best advocates.

Just as each child is unique, each family situation is unique. Dr. Trunzo's best advice to families: "Don't wait until you are in a crisis to seek help. Anticipate problems by paying attention to the warning signs." He went on to say there are positive ways to get help from resources such as the Internet, books, physicians, teachers, friends, and family.

Being in a much healthier place now, I was able to look at what we had been through as a family. Dr. Trunzo believes that the whole family unit needs to be addressed when treating a child. This belief was what I had felt that day in his office. Through our consultation, he saw that everybody in our family was hurting, and we needed to decompress before we could begin to heal. It was his caring approach that touched this tired mom's heart.

3

The World of Behavioral Therapy

The next day I made the call to Dr. Roger M. Martig, a licensed clinical psychologist in private practice. In addition to twenty-five years of professional counseling and teaching experience, Dr. Martig is also a consulting psychologist for the Maricopa County Juvenile Court Center. It was the first time that I had called an office and felt better simply by listening to the voice-mail message.

This was not a typical answering machine message. Several of my questions were answered within minutes by a calm, efficient female voice. The recording gave me three options. First, if I had a concern, I could leave my name and number for Dr. Martig to return my call. Second, if I was a first-time caller, I could learn more information about Dr. Martig by pressing "2." And third, if I wanted to listen to Dr. Martig's mental-health tips of the month, I could press "3." Of course, I selected all three options. After leaving my name and number, I hung up, already feeling the benefits of psychotherapy.

Filled with renewed hope for a possible solution, we went into this treatment with a sincere desire to help Ian. Unlike our previous experience with therapy, this one was much less intimidating. In fact, upon meeting Dr. Martig, we felt as if we were simply sharing our story with someone who was very interested, in a relaxed, nonthreatening atmosphere.

We made a standing weekly appointment to see Dr. Martig. For the first half hour we talked together: the doctor, my son, my husband, and I. For the next half hour, Dr. Martig met alone with Ian while Roger and I waited in the next room. As we sat in the adjoining waiting room, we could hear muffled conversation through the door. Not one to leave my son during any type of medical visit, I felt some anxiety over that closed door. After all, we had just met this new doctor. However, the sounds of a mini-basketball thumping against the wall, along with that conversation, put me more at ease. That, coupled with the fact that every few minutes I found myself with my ear close to the door.

Looking back, we were not comfortable talking about the past week's problems with Ian in the room. Roger was especially concerned about discussing issues while Ian listened, at times smirking as we recounted the misery of the incidents he had caused. Yet Dr. Martig wanted to see the interaction between us and observe our son's antagonism. I believe he also wanted to see our family as a unit and how we interacted.

I've since discovered that one of the strategies recommended with oppositional defiant children is not let them see you upset. You don't want them to believe they're controlling you and your emotions. My husband's instincts were right on the mark about that.

During one especially tough visit, Dr. Martig commented to Ian, "You seem to be glad you make your mom cry." Ian simply shrugged his shoulders and scowled. He slouched in his chair and avoided eye contact. In the early days of therapy, he would refuse to get into the car to go every week. It was a physical and mental struggle to get him into the car, and then once we arrived at the office, it was another struggle to get him to walk into the office. Imagine two adults in the medical complex parking lot, car door open, waiting for a defiant boy to join them. This at the end of a busy workday for us and a school day for Ian. Talk about stressed-out families! We found ourselves talking, threatening, begging, and simply waiting for him to come on his own accord. It was not successful. I admit to dragging him out of the car in desperation on several occasions. It was an ugly, exhausting process. I believed it was necessary.

We soon learned that Dr. Martig's treatment methods were eclectic and included play therapy and reality therapy approaches. In

Ian's situation, he used play therapy, as it so nicely fit in with Ian's love of sports. The doctor would let Ian shoot hoops with a small basketball as they talked about things. It was a relaxing, nonthreatening way to open up the dialogue. It worked well. We also learned a new term to use with Ian. Rather than using "time-out," we would call it time in the "penalty box," putting it on his level of understanding. High stick a guy in hockey and you're going to get time in the penalty box. I liked the analogy. We've used it ever since.

Over the course of five months, we began to see positive changes. Ian didn't seem quite as angry. Through conversations and even drawings, he expressed that he feels small when he's angry. I still have the colored drawing in which the doctor asked him to draw himself happy on one side of the paper and angry on the other half. Doctor Martig pointed out to us that the happy boy is much bigger while the angry boy is small. That's how our son was feeling. He was beginning to communicate. We were making progress.

Marriage and Family Dynamics

The old saying is, "You don't know someone until you've lived with them." As parents of a son with ODD, I rewrote that saying to, "You don't know yourself or your spouse until you've lived with seemingly insurmountable challenges." I discovered things about myself I would rather not have known. I saw sides of my husband I would rather not have seen. Had we been going along smoothly with well-adjusted children, we never would have seen the dark, despairing sides of each other. And it wasn't pretty.

Children with ODD generate strong feelings in people. One of the most common characteristics of ODD is the practice of annoying people while enjoying their reactions. We were no exception. Ian became a master at inciting conflict between my husband and me, while taking the focus off himself. In addition to the daily struggles of life with ODD, my marriage was being tested again and again. The situation had affected every relationship in our family and the very structure of our marriage.

During our behavioral therapy sessions, Roger and I took some time to talk with Dr. Martig about our relationship. On top of dealing with years of Ian's struggles, we also were dealing with relocation, new careers, our adolescent daughter's needs, and a host of other life situations. It was essential to keep the lines of communication open between the two of us. It was a struggle.

At the doctor's request, we brought our daughter to one of the sessions. At twelve years old and going through the tough time of adolescence, Abby was also struggling. After some small talk, the focus of conversation turned to her. Abby's turmoil was one of the hardest things I've witnessed. At that point, years of suppressed emotion and anger came pouring out. She could hardly speak through her tears and sobs. My heart felt that familiar pull as I watched her pain. To my amazement, she was able to communicate how she felt. Yet did she really understand her feelings? How could she? I'm an adult and at times I can't sort it all out. I kept reminding myself that it was because she loved her brother that she felt so hurt by him. My mission was to help their relationship heal. Every mother wants her children to be there for each other, support each other, and above all, love each other.

Wild Horses

During one of our weekly therapy visits, Dr. Martig explained that Ian was like a thoroughbred racehorse: he was driven. This reminded me of the pediatrician who had said our son was going to be a strong leader someday. What both of these respected doctors pointed out held no importance to me. What my son was going to be when he grew up was secondary to who he was going to be. Was he going to be a man of integrity or of deceit? Was he going to be compassionate or mean spirited? Was he going to be gentle or violent? And how could we help him to become the man God intended him to be?

My son may have been like a thoroughbred, but at the moment, he was a thoroughbred running wild and out of control. Besides, I'm not much for horse racing anyway.

If the Shoe Fits

During the time we were still in treatment with Dr. Martig, Ian and I went shopping. I'd learned with Ian that it was best to avoid going shopping together. I'd discovered that he was becoming extremely materialistic, and going into a store brought him to the edge. There was simply too much sensory input from noise, people, and things. Unfortunately, at times he had to go with me, such as when he needed new tennis shoes.

As we drove to the store, he informed me that he wanted to get the exact same shoes he already had, only in a bigger size. There was one problem: What were the chances the store where we were going would have that shoe in that size? Trying to defuse the potential crisis, I explained that if this store didn't have his shoes we could either pick another pair or go to another store the next day. Knowing what was bound to happen, I felt that familiar sense of dread coming on.

The friendly young salesman approached us and asked how he could help. I silently wished he really could help! After giving him our selection, he disappeared behind the wall to check on available sizes. "No, I'm sorry, we don't have that size. Would you like to try another pair?" It was all over. No, actually, it was just beginning.

I looked at Ian, and he was jeering at me. He started to walk away. As I joined him, he stopped walking. He started muttering, "Stupid! I hate this!" I encouraged him to come with me and assured him that we would check with the other store tomorrow. It was getting late, and after another trying day I just wanted to head home. Ian had other plans.

He deliberately walked through the store at a snail's pace. I went on ahead toward the car. By the time he caught up to me, he was in a rage. I avoided talking to him or looking at him and started the car. He slammed the rear door with all his might and proceeded to start kicking the back of my seat violently. All the built-up anticipation of getting new shoes, his exact shoes in a bigger size, and the disappointment that followed were more than he could process. He was out of control, and we were forty minutes from home.

I continued to ignore him and began the drive out of the busy parking lot. His kicks became harder and his screaming louder. He was spitting out hateful words and punching the seat. That was it.

In the middle of an aisle, I slammed on the brakes, put the car in park, and jumped out. What follows is an example of a mom driven to her own tantrum after living years of it with her child. I threw open the rear door and got into his face.

His red, tear-streaked face looked at me defiantly, as if to say, "Come on! What are you going to do?" He wanted to fight. I screamed, "Knock it off!" and proceeded to tell him to either stop what he was doing or get out of my car. It was my car and he had no right to do what he was doing. As I was yelling in the middle of the busy parking lot, I noticed a man in a car had slowed down and, with his window down, was looking at me.

Facing him, I yelled, "What? Do you want to take over here? You try this!" He quickly rolled up his window and drove off. And after my own episode, Ian settled down and we drove off. So much for thoroughbred horses.

We Had Seen Better Days

After months of weekly therapy sessions and noticeable improvements in Ian's behavior, we decided to start weaning him off the sessions. Dr. Martig suggested that, rather than simply stopping, we cut back to twice a month. Then our visits dropped to once a month. Finally we agreed we were ready to go solo. That and our insurance coverage on psychotherapy visits was maxed out. (The financial aspects of helping a troubled child is another topic.) I'm confident, however, that Dr. Martig, as would most other respected psychologists, would have worked out a payment plan of some sort for us.

With some trepidation, we stopped behavioral therapy after five months. Ian seemed happier, better able to control his anger and express his feelings. We had definitely made progress and were feeling confident that we were going forward. If only it had lasted.

After a few months, the old behaviors began to re-emerge. Ian was easily irritated, easily frustrated, and growing more violent. He was acting out toward Abby now as well. I continued to bear the brunt of most of his outbursts, but anyone who was in his path felt the stress. Before it got too bad, we decided to resume therapy to find our way back. I called Dr. Martig.

This time, however, Ian seemed to look forward to visiting with the doctor—almost too much. In hindsight, I believe Ian viewed Dr. Martig as a buddy to play games with. He didn't have many friends because of his temperament, and his own family was pretty weary of his outbursts. After several sessions, we felt like we weren't making any progress. We weren't seeing the same improvements in Ian's behavior as we had before. It wouldn't be until later, while talking with Dr. Martig, that I discovered why.

Different People, Different Results

I've learned that these children are often led to despair by feelings of not being understood by anyone. They give up hope of being understood and grow angrier. In fact, it is this feeling of being misunderstood that leads a child to feel let down by the adults who care for him. This is where the hostility comes in. These children feel that, in order to prove their own adequacy, they must prove everyone else around them to be inadequate. This is perceived as a conscious and willful act on the part of the child, when in fact it is not. It is a coping mechanism for dealing with constant pain and distress.

Through therapy, Ian became aware of how his destructive behavior was affecting his own life and the lives of his family. He learned how to express what he was feeling inside, especially the anger and hostility. It was the first time I can recall Ian actually telling me, "You made me mad, Mom!" In the past he would simply act on that feeling; now he was telling me how I made him feel. That

35

was progress. In my heart I also knew he needed something more. But what exactly was it? It was still eluding us.

During this second round of therapy, Roger and I the opportunity to discuss our marriage and family situation. Dr. Martig felt that perhaps Ian was sensing the discontent between us as a couple and playing on that. That really came as no surprise. Dr. Martig was right.

There were occasions that I'd take Ian to the appointment by myself. It was then that I had the opportunity to talk with Dr. Martig one on one while Ian played games in the waiting room. This was a real gift to me. As a wife and mother I had been so busy caring for my family that I spent little time caring for myself. With the demands of a challenging child, his needs and the needs of everyone else came first. Along the way, I watched as my own relationships with friends and family disintegrated. I simply had neither the time nor the energy to invest in relationships. Goals and dreams? Gone. At least for now. My main focus was my family. And getting my son the help he needed.

With Dr. Martig's encouragement, I began looking at myself as an individual again, not in a self-absorbed sort of way but in a healthy way. I had a lot to offer and gifts to share with others. It had been so long since I thought of those things that I had almost forgotten them. I used to have treasured women friends. I used to go to the theater occasionally. I used to work outside the home in a creative job I enjoyed. My husband and I used to enjoy traveling. I didn't want to continue living this life of "used to do things" anymore. I wanted to start participating in life again, no matter the circumstances I found myself in. I made the decision to start caring for myself again and growing as an individual. It wasn't going to be easy but it was necessary to my survival.

While conducting research for this book, I talked with Dr. Martig about the effects of both brief and long-term psychotherapy on individuals. He stated, "The real benefit of long-term psychotherapy is the durability of it. You'll see it in a variety of little ways throughout your days. This is true for most people, not all people. Some individuals, for unknown reasons, seem to zone out to it." He went on to say that, years later, people will think about some aspect of what they had learned about themselves, about relating to others, or about simply getting along, that they had discovered in therapy. It's those little nuggets of insight that we benefit from.

I believe that our time spent in therapy with Dr. Martig was very helpful to Ian. It was the first time Ian really made an emotional connection to a doctor. Someone really listened to him and made him feel understood.

Our next stop on this journey: back to our trusted pediatrician.

Looking for Another Avenue

Dr. Trunzo knew from our first visit that we wanted to exhaust every avenue before resorting to medication. Were we missing something? Had we done all we could do to help Ian? I felt that, if we went with medication, we would be giving up and taking an easy way out. Dr. Trunzo sensed this and was supportive as he gave us yet another referral, this time to a specialist in pediatric neuropsychology. He agreed that further testing would be a good idea.

Pediatric Neuropsychology

After years of behavioral therapy, pediatricians, and family doctors, we decided to seek further help. The behavioral approach worked at times, but overall the behavioral spikes of highs and lows kept recurring. Pediatric neuropsychology sounded impressive, yet after all we'd been through we approached this doctor with guarded enthusiasm.

What exactly is pediatric neuropsychology all about? Neuropsychology is the study of brain-behavior relationships. Individuals having trouble with cognitive tasks such as attention, concentration, memory or problem solving, due to disease or a developmental problem, may benefit from having a neuropsychological evaluation. Through this evaluation, the doctor can gain insight into a person's cognitive functioning (related to thinking or knowing). Furthermore, the evaluation provides information on how a person is relating in social and emotional situations.

The doctor gathers information about a person's developmental, medical, academic, and behavioral history. In addition, information is collected through direct observation and neuropsychological testing. Certain tests are chosen depending on the individual's history. A typical evaluation includes assessments of the following:

- *general intellectual functioning*
- *academic achievement*
- *attention and executive functions*
- *learning and memory*
- *language functions*
- *sensorimotor functions*
- *visuospatial functions*
- *social and emotional functioning*

Our goal was to simply find out if Ian had something going on physically or neurologically. So we signed up for eight hours of neuropsychological evaluations. It sounded intense, and at times it was; however, these tests also included several fun activities like puzzles, games, and computer skills. Thankfully, all this was broken up into two four-hour appointments on consecutive Saturday mornings.

I think completing the medical history forms alone took an hour. Besides the standard health history, I was completing several parent rating scales on Ian's behavior. It seemed a never-ending task. I was beginning to resent filling out all the paperwork. I looked over at Roger and knew what he was thinking; he had expressed it before. Why are we spending a Saturday here? Ian should be outside, playing and having fun. Why? We were there to find out exactly why. We were there for some answers.

We began by explaining that Ian lacked self-control, withheld affection, hid his feelings, was easily frustrated, was often angry and defiant, overreacted when facing a problem, and showed little remorse for his actions. He also seemed unaffected by negative consequences. For example, if he was planning to attend his friend's birthday party at three o'clock and he was on the edge of a meltdown, verbal warnings of missing the party were ineffective. Can't go to the party this year? So what. I'll go to his party next year. I don't care. Getting ready to go to a new movie with the family? Ian began to lose control and would go into a rage. When I warned him that we wouldn't be going to the show if he didn't calm down, he would scream that he didn't care about the stupid show! There was nothing I could take away or deny Ian that would appear to have an impact on his behavior. He said he did not care. I believed him.

Ian's lack of remorse for his actions concerned me a great deal. I found it frightening that he simply didn't care how his behaviors affected others in our family.

Several tests were administered to Ian including: Wechsler Abbreviated Scale of Intelligence (WASI), Wechsler Individual Achievement Test—Second Edition (WIAT-II) Abbreviated; Children's Memory Scale (CMS); Integrated Visual and Auditory Continuous Performance Test (IVA-CPT); Trailmaking Tests; Wisconsin Card Sorting Test; Behavioral Rating Inventory of Executive Function (BRIEF); and Behavior Assessment System for Children (BASC) Parent Rating Scales.

Throughout the evaluation, Ian was cooperative and did his personal best. The doctor expressed surprise at Ian's behavioral history. He had trouble with the fact that in school, sports, and social settings, Ian did well. It was at home that he became defiant and out of control. As other doctors had told us, this doctor said that usually the behavior spills over into other areas of Ian's life, especially school. What I was about to learn, after further research, was that one indicator of ODD is just that: children are able to sit still and perform well outside the home. It's when they are home in their own environment that the defiant behavior emerges.

Again, as in the previous therapy sessions, this doctor preferred Ian to be in the room when we were discussing his behavior and the results of the testing. Looking back, I am reminded of the main characteristic of oppositional defiance: children believe they are our equals and they like to know they're getting to us. It makes them feel like they are in control. Having Ian in the room with us as we discussed the test results and our home situation was not the correct approach for dealing with a child struggling with defiance.

This is one of the most baffling and frustrating aspects of ODD for me: Ian can maintain his composure and perform well with others, yet at home he is a totally different person. How often have I heard the positive feedback? I've been told how polite he is, how well he follows directions, and how he is a good sport. I've discovered this is where the isolation of ODD comes in for parents. Others just don't see the challenges we face each day. In fact, if we even hinted that our child was less than exemplary, we would quickly pick up on the disbelief of the adult we were talking to. I've had friends comment that, while Ian may be active and at times difficult, he's a typical boy. These comments were followed by one of those smiles. You know them. The smile that says, "You're exaggerating. He's a great kid." Well, yes, he is a great kid. And no, I am not exaggerating. That's where the conversations about our special child end. We shut down the lines of communication. Other people simply don't know the situation, and I don't have the energy to help them understand. The isolation grows.

After two consecutive Saturdays in the neuropsychologist's office, we had a six- page report on our son. Included in the results were intellectual functioning (IQ), screening of academic achievements, assessment of memory functions, and assessment of attention and concentration. While all the results ranked average to high average, the parent behavior ratings showed evidence of problems with regard to emotional control, behavior, and adaptability. As a result, the doctor recommended treatment: a behavior modification program. Although I respected his opinion, I knew we would not be going that route again. It did not work. At least it did not work alone. We needed more than behavior plans. We had to get to the root of the problem before we could move forward.

The Dance of Defiance

The doctor gave us a handout entitled "Emotional Control" which listed behavior modification strategies and interventions. Several years ago, this may have been appreciated. However, we had tried every tip on that sheet with no success. Again, I felt like professionals were not listening to me. If he truly understood what we had been talking about regarding our son over the last two weeks, he would also have understood that the strategies listed on that handout did not apply to Ian. In fact, it was almost insulting to us as parents to receive this, as if we hadn't tried these methods already! I am grateful though, for what the doctor did give us: a diagnosis. For the first time in over seven years of searching, we had a name for the problem we were facing: oppositional defiant disorder. Being able to put a name to the problem made it seem so much more manageable. We would take it from here. Right back to our trusted pediatrician, Dr. Trunzo.

4

What Is Oppositional Defiant Disorder?

The American Psychiatric Association's *Diagnostic and Statistical Manual of Mental Health Disorders, Fourth Edition, Text Revision (DSM-IV-TR)* defines oppositional defiant disorder as a pattern of negativistic, hostile, and defiant behavior lasting at least 6 months, during which four (or more) of the following are present:

- *Often loses temper*
- *Often argues with adults*
- *Often actively defies or refuses to comply with adults' requests or rules*
- *Often deliberately annoys people*
- *Often blames others for own mistakes or misbehavior*
- *Is "touchy" or easily annoyed by others*
- *Is often angry or resentful*
- *Is often spiteful or vindictive*

  Negativistic and defiant behaviors are expressed by persistent stubbornness, resistance to directions, and unwillingness to compromise, give in, or negotiate with adults or peers. Defiance may also include deliberate or persistent testing of limits, or by verbal aggression (usually without the more serious physical aggression

*seen in Conduct Disorder). Usually individuals with
this disorder do not regard themselves as oppositional
or defiant, but justify their behavior as a response to
unreasonable demands or circumstances (p.100)*.

As the *DSM-IV-TR* points out, we usually see this defiance at
home, "Manifestations of the disorder are almost invariably present
in the home setting, but may not be evident at school or in the
community" (p. 100). Hence our feelings of inadequacy as parents!
I'm sure you've heard the comments. After a birthday party: "Your
son is so polite!" In parent-teacher conferences: "He is a pleasure to
have in class!" No wonder we are baffled as parents of children with
oppositional defiant disorder.

In his book, *The Defiant Child: a Parent's Guide to Oppositional
Defiant Disorder*, Douglas A. Riley identifies this common theme
among children with ODD: "The dominant thoughts of the ODD
child revolve around defeating anyone's attempt to exercise authority
over them" (p. 3). Simple tasks will often be seen by the defiant child
as a form of manipulation on the part of the adult. These thoughts
cause parents and families to constantly be on guard against even
remotely appearing to be controlling. This means anticipating the
child's reactions ahead of time. Everything from "Please close the
door" to "Please brush your teeth" becomes suspect. Before long,
everyone involved feels the stress of "walking on eggs" around this
child.

Parents find themselves being manipulated and bullied into
doing things to avoid a confrontation. These things start out small,
such as allowing 10 more minutes of computer time, but eventually
they become bigger. We begin to find ourselves doing unbelievable
things to keep our child from a meltdown.

An informative website, www.notmykid.org gives parents of children with ODD credit for what they're dealing with. It acknowledges
that raising a child with ODD can be frustrating and exhausting.

---

*Reprinted with permission from the Diagnostic and Statistical Manual of Mental Disorders,
Copyright 2000. American Psychiatric Association.

Parents may become isolated and feel helpless. The website points out that:

Children with ODD are much more difficult to be with than other children of their age. The destructiveness and disagreeableness are purposeful. Every request can end up as a power struggle. Perhaps hardest of all to bear, they rarely are truly sorry and often believe nothing is their fault.

It's Not That Simple...There's More

Oppositional defiant disorder rarely occurs alone. The child usually has another neuropsychiatric disorder in addition to ODD, referred to as a hidden disorder. When disorders occur together, it's called comorbidity. The area of comorbidity in pediatric medicine is an important area of research being conducted today. Rather than seeking one primary diagnosis, parents need to look at all aspects of the child's behavior.

To add to the challenge, here are some common examples of comorbid combinations with ODD: ODD plus ADHD, ODD plus depression/anxiety, and ODD plus learning disabilities (LD). In our case, we discovered after further neurological evaluation, that Ian was experiencing depression, anxiety, and obsessive-compulsive symptoms. It was a year after the ODD diagnosis that we learned Ian was being oppositional as a way of coping with the other disorders.

What Is Attention Deficit Hyperactivity Disorder?

According to the American Academy of Pediatrics, attention deficit hyperactivity disorder (ADHD) is one of the most common chronic conditions of childhood, affecting 4 to 12 percent of school-aged children. It is approximately three times more likely to occur in boys than in girls. ADHD is difficult to diagnose in children under five, since many behaviors they exhibit are normal for their developmental age. In addition, preschoolers are physically growing and

45

changing rapidly. As with preschoolers, teenagers also display behaviors that are normal for their developmental age. They too, are physically going through many changes.

The American Academy of Pediatrics has developed diagnosis guidelines for children ages six to twelve. There are three symptoms of ADHD: inattention, hyperactivity, and impulsivity. A child may have one or more of these symptoms and are classified as follows:

1. Inattentive. Children with this type of ADHD often appear to be daydreaming or simply not paying attention in class. Their symptoms oftentimes go unnoticed until other signs of trouble appear. Interestingly, this is the most common type of ADHD in girls.

2. Hyperactive/Impulsive. Often referred to by parents as the "Energizer Bunny" syndrome. Kids are superactive, have a hard time staying in their seat, and appear fidgety. They often speak out without thinking and interrupt others. These children can, however, pay attention.

3. Combined Inattentive/Hyperactive/Impulsive. These children exhibit all three symptoms; this is the most common type of ADHD.

While there is no single test for a diagnosis of ADHD, a pediatrician can determine whether or not a child has the disorder by a variety of evaluations. These include a complete medical history; a thorough physical exam; information from parents, schools, and caregivers; and given assessments and evaluations. The doctor will also examine the developmental behavior of the child in relation to his or her peers. Are most other kids this age displaying these types of behaviors?

Most important, the doctor will talk with the child. How the doctor talks to the child is as important as what he or she actually says. A safe, nonthreatening atmosphere will help the child open up and discuss feelings, fears, and questions. Self-esteem is a big issue for these kids. They are often frustrated, unhappy, and misunderstood. The good news is, that while ADHD may be challenging to diagnose, there is treatment available to help. Parents and pediatricians can work together to form a team of professionals to help a child with ADHD. This team can develop a treatment plan including behavior therapy, medication, education, parenting classes, and counseling. As with ODD, it may be necessary to try a number of strategies before finding the right combination for your child. The key is being persistent and not giving up. Remember, we are our child's best advocate.

In *Understanding ADHD: Information for Parents About Attention Deficit Hyperactivity Disorder* the American Academy of Pediatrics discusses coexisting conditions among children who have been diagnosed with ADHD. These common coexisting conditions include the following: oppositional defiant disorder or conduct disorder, mood disorders/depression, anxiety disorders, and learning disabilities. There is an obvious pattern here. These coexisting conditions occur in a variety of disorders. As with ADHD, it is critical to look for coexisting disorders when examining a child with ODD since effective treatments depend on an accurate diagnosis.

Educational Implications

Under the *Individuals with Disabilities Education Act (IDEA)*, students do not currently qualify for special-education services based solely on a diagnosis of oppositional defiant disorder. However, if parents believe their child has a learning disability, perhaps as a coexisting disorder with ODD, they may request that a comprehensive evaluation be conducted by the public school. This free evaluation is the first step in collecting information and input from parents and staff about a child's learning needs. This process may include social, psychological, and educational assessments to determine the need for special-education services. It uses observation, testing, and test analysis to determine students' strengths as well as weaknesses. Parents must give consent before the evaluation begins.

The second step in the process is determining the eligibility of a student. A team—composed of educators, administrators, agency personnel, and parents—reviews the evaluations and existing data and determines if the student is eligible for special-education services. It's important to view the teachers and staff at the school as our allies. Keeping the lines of communication open and staying informed help us to be our child's best advocate in education.

An important piece of the puzzle in raising children with ODD and other disorders is understanding the educational process. In our case, Ian's oppositional defiance was not interfering with his learning process. I did not observe any signs of a learning disability during our struggles. However, his defiant behavior was spilling over into the classroom, and I knew it wouldn't be long before his education was negatively affected.

As our journey unfolded, it wasn't until I confided in my son's teacher that we found the right path. I've since learned that school psychologists and teachers are a valuable resource to parents. In fact, the classroom teacher is often the first to identify a problem with a child and often becomes an advocate for that student. However, teachers can only help us if we let them in.

Strategies for Teachers

In *Exceptional Learners: An Introduction to Special Education, Ninth Edition,* strategies are given for teachers of students with ODD. One example truly illustrates the challenge of working with these children. Daniel is a student who repeatedly pulled displays off the walls in the hallway. After several warnings against this behavior, he lost recess time. He still continued the behavior, ending up in the principal's office.

The teacher tells of the day Daniel walked down the hall and did not pull down one single display. The teacher, in front of the class, praised him for his excellent behavior. This sent him into a rage; the other students watched as Daniel ran down the hallway tearing down every display he could get his hands on.

Positive reinforcement, a successful behavior modification strategy used by parents and educators alike, backfired with Daniel. Students without ODD would likely have responded favorably by the teacher's public praise. However, Daniel saw it as controlling his behavior. As discussed earlier, a common characteristic of children with ODD is the desire to not be controlled by authority. The primary response of a child with ODD is public opposition. Rather than using positive reinforcement, parents and teachers need to use "indirect reinforcement." It's pretty clear how mentally tiring this can be for both teachers and parents.

Suggestions for indirect reinforcement include minimizing public praise. Instead, the teacher could tap the student on the shoulder, whisper praise, leave notes, or provide rewards discreetly. This avoids the controlling feeling brought on by public praise.

Daniel was demonstrating another common characteristic of children with ODD: difficulty remembering how to respond when frustrated and trouble recalling the consequences of previous explosive episodes. Simply put, Daniel didn't remember how to act appropriately when he became frustrated. He also didn't remember the consequences of his actions. Even if those consequences repeatedly landed him in the principal's office.

One of the most helpful resources I've found as a teacher comes in the form of a deck of cards! It's called "You Can Handle Them All: A Quick-Action Card Deck," and it is published by The Master Teacher, Inc. Described as "A Quick-Reference Guide for Handling 117 Different Misbehaviors at School and at Home," I keep it handy. These cards list descriptions of behavior; primary cause(s) of misbehavior; methods, procedures, and techniques to employ immediately; and mistakes to avoid. In working with a student with defiant behavior, for example, I would look at the card titled, "The Defier." This particular card lists nine techniques to employ when working with this student. In reviewing strategies for teachers, I believe the following are excellent tips:

- *Build a strong rapport with the student.*

- *Never get into a "yes you will" contest. Silence is a better response.*

- *Don't take the defiance personally.*

- *Use the "Delayed Teacher Response" when a student refuses to cooperate. Don't say anything right away.*

- *Be caring, honest, and respectful.*

- *Give the student some classroom responsibilities.*

- *Provide quiet space, away from others. This must be at the student's request.*

- *Work with the student to form an agreement about how you will treat each other.*

- *Provide structure. It is essential to know what is expected and what the routines and procedures are.*

Of course, I would add: Offer positive reinforcement in the form of discreet praise. For example, a nod and smile, a quick "good job" whispered as you walk by, or a "thumbs up" when other students aren't looking. The key is to avoid public praise.

As a teacher, somewhere along the way I heard the following saying which I've taken to heart: Students don't care what you know until they know that you care. That is such a powerful statement for me as both a teacher and a mother. It is one of my top recommended strategies for working with children with ODD. Building a strong rapport with the child is the first step in showing that you indeed care. In addition, these children must be treated fairly; break the rules and you will see defiance at its best. This isn't always easy in a class-room of thirty students, but it is well worth the effort.

Strategies for Parents

Throughout this journey, I have searched for ways to help Ian and my family overcome the obstacles of oppositional defiant disorder. I've discovered many helpful strategies along the way. However, I found that for any strategy to be successful, I had to be in a healthy place before I could implement it. I needed to be emotionally, physically, and spiritually able to start a strategy and see it through. I held on to the following verse from Psalm 46:10: "Be still, and know that I am God." Once I was in a good place, I could approach my son and be more effective.

I found the following tips to be especially helpful in raising a child with ODD, and they work well with coexisting disorders such as ADHD, anxiety, and learning disorders. Oppositional behavior is fueled by competition. Sibling rivalry is competitive to begin with. Adding oppositional defiance to sibling rivalry is a recipe for conflict. Parents must advocate for all children in the household. Working to avoid competition in the home is essential. Giving them coping skills will help siblings growing up with the challenges of a brother or sister with ODD. This brings us to strategies for parents:

- *Avoid giving ultimatums. You will lose.*

- *Avoid competition. As stated, sibling rivalry is competitive to begin with. Avoid adding to it by bringing competition into the home. The result will be poor winners and poor losers. And lots of resentment on both sides.*

- *Model coping skills for all children in the home. For example, do not advise the siblings to simply "ignore" the hostile behavior; it will not go away. Children with ODD will simply increase the behavior until they get the attention being sought.*

- *Decrease distractions. Video arcades, computer games, interactive video games, TV, and music can be too stimulating. During homework and discussions, it is very helpful to turn off music and television.*

- *Reward positive behavior. Indirect, positive reinforce-*

ments, such as whispered kind words, a tap on the shoulder, or other discreet forms of praise work effectively with defiant children. The key term here, with ODD, is discreet praise.

- Get organized. Keeping things organized, from your household to your child's backpack, will help reduce frustration when completing tasks. Providing a neat, quiet, organized homework area, for example, limits distractions and helps children focus on learning.

- Keep it simple. Give one or two requests at a time to avoid overwhelming your child. Rattling off a list of things to do not only frustrates a child but also leads to dismal results.

- Set realistic goals. Give plenty of opportunities for your child to feel successful. Take one baby step at a time. Realize that moving forward and seeing results one day may not mean the next day will go as well. Celebrate even the smallest victories.

- Give time to make transitions. In other words, our children need time to "switch gears," from one activity to another. Allow time for them to make that change.

- Limit choices. Our children don't need to have five choices of beverages to drink during dinner. Milk or water? Keep it simple! Giving too many choices only leads to struggles, frustration, and poor decisions. Give your child two to three choices at a time. The fewer the better.

In reviewing these tips, one particular memory came to mind, regarding distractions. I sure learned a lesson from this one! It was Ian's eighth birthday, and we wanted to celebrate by hosting a bowling party with his friends. It was one of those "cosmic" parties, in which the lights went out and colorful spotlights encircled the bowling alley. In addition, large screens scrolled down above each lane, playing very loud, colorful music videos. As if that weren't enough, throughout the party, drawings were held, names were called over the loud speaker, and the birthday boy got to play games for prizes.

How is that for limiting distractions? Needless to say, it wasn't long into the party before we realized we had made a big mistake. It was a very stressful two hours, during which we worked tirelessly to keep Ian from a meltdown and the party running smoothly. It was our last bowling party.

Strategies for Spouses

Children who are oppositional will often manipulate parents to get what they want. They are masters at putting Mom and Dad at odds with one another. Remember, the child with ODD believes that he or she is an equal to parents and not subject to their authority. This brings us to strategies for spouses:

- *Present a united front with your child. United, we stand; divided, we fall.*

- *Discuss discipline plans privately; share in being the disciplinarian.*

- *Be consistent. Say what you mean and mean what you say.*

- *Watch your spouse for signs of fatigue; be ready to take over.*

- *Plan some time for yourself and time for each other, even if it's a trip to the ice cream store for a sundae.*

- *Give each other space to unwind. Conversation isn't always necessary. Simply being there for each other is all we need.*

- *Watch for signs that other children in the family need*

your time and attention. Give them your time, support, and love. Help fill in the gaps.

- *Show your child that your spouse deserves respect at all times. Stand up for each other in the battles.*

- *Walk away.*

It is imperative that parents present a united front with their children. One tiny chink in the armor and it's all over. Our defiant children know how exhausted we are. They use that to their advantage. Mom won't let Andrew play outside; go ask Dad. Dad says Andrew cannot buy a new DVD movie at the store; go ask Mom. Better yet, tell Mom that Dad said it was a good idea. Now the battle is set. The defiant child has set the parents up for failure or at least another heated argument.

Parents must discuss strategies and approaches privately. While it is all right to disagree about the course of action, spouses need to make decisions together and stick with them in dealing with their child. Being consistent in your approach is essential. We know this is a good strategy in raising any child. I know from experience that it's not an option when dealing with an oppositional, defiant child.

To avoid one spouse's becoming burned out, it's important to be active in sharing the role of discipline. If you see your husband becoming frustrated, it may be time for him to step away and recharge. Take over and give him a break. Likewise, if you see your wife struggling to balance it all and handle a defiant child, reach out to help her before she collapses. It's also important to be aware of the needs of your other children. So often we are consumed with our role as caregivers that we miss events going on in our other children's lives.

Whether it's an hour in a coffee shop or a week in paradise, time alone with your spouse is vital. I'm aware that even an hour-long break may be impossible at times. It's important to not give up on the idea. Start off slowly, maybe while a neighbor watches your child for that hour. It's amazing the benefits you will reap from that time. We must model respect to our children by supporting each other in the face of all adversity.

Finally, when I repeatedly found myself locked in the destructive cycle of anger, rage, and brewing violence, I began to simply walk away. Knowing that Ian was spinning out of control, and beyond reason, the best I could do was to leave the situation until it spent itself. Whether it was a confrontation between him and me or one involving other family members, I would seek refuge in—of all places—my closet.

In my walk-in closet, I have just enough space for a small chair. To the left of the door, and next to my hanging sweaters, skirts, and slacks, sits a southern plantation chair that dates back to 1835. This antique chair has a rounded back with intricate carvings and arms that embrace me while I'm sitting in it.

I've come to call it my "prayer chair." I alternate between calling it that and calling it my "crying chair." I've done plenty of both—praying and crying—in that chair. Imagine what that chair has seen over the past 100 years! I know that, since it has occupied my closet, it has seen anger, despair, fear, and frustration. It's also seen a woman deep in prayer, gaining hope, and drawing on faith. Sitting in that antique chair has given me a sense of comfort, longevity, and perseverance. Just a little time in the closet, a refuge from the raging storm.

5

Matters of the Heart

This area is a tender one for me to bring to mind and put to words. I've tried to file the memory away and not revisit it. But it's important to see how far we've come and to count the blessings we now have. In order to do that, sometimes we have to go back.

Often, when I meet someone new, they reply that we must not have much sibling rivalry since the children are six years apart. Well, of course, they don't know the half of it! But in fairness to them, one wouldn't think rivalry would be a big issue. With us, though, it was a redefined sibling rivalry.

It began at the dinner table on Valentine's Day with our then five-year-old daughter, Abby. Among the paper hearts and home-made valentines, chocolate hearts and cut out cupids, we gave her the exciting news that she would become a big sister! She recently had begun to notice that, while most of her friends had brothers and sisters, she didn't. It was a topic she brought up more and more often. When we told her, her precious reply was "Oh, that's the answer to my prayer!" What an appropriate and sweet celebration to have on Valentine's Day! I hurried to write her response in her baby journal I had been keeping. This little boy couldn't have been more wanted or born into a family that loved him any more than we did!

Fast forward seven years. This precious daughter was now twelve years old and emotionally wounded by her beloved baby brother. By the time Ian was seven, after years of therapy and doctor visits, tears and challenges, our family wasn't what that little five-year-old girl had in mind that Valentine's Day. And it broke our hearts. Like all moms, in my heart I hold a desire for my children to love each other. This wasn't the family I had envisioned either. There had to be a way to make things better. What an appropriate symbol for our broken hearts, the tie-in with our Valentine's Day announcement just a few years before.

A most poignant memory comes to mind. It had been an especially challenging day, filled with episodes of rage and lots of trials. This was during a period when we were in behavioral therapy with Ian. We hadn't started any medications yet. I was so tired of the tension, anger, and constant squabbling. I'd had enough. That evening, I called my children into the living room for a family meeting. The four of us had a heartbreaking few minutes which I will never forget. Ian flatly refused to sit down in the room and instead stood around the corner within earshot. Abby sat and sobbed when I demanded that she and her brother treat each other with love and respect. I lectured on being each other's ally and sticking up for each other. I reminded them that we were a family, and families take care of each other. At this point, the dam broke.

Through her tears, she expressed the raw emotions that she had been hiding. She sobbed, "He has ruined our family. Every special occasion is ruined with his tantrums. We can't do anything! We don't go anywhere. I hate it! He ruins holidays. I do not love him." I can still picture her tormented expression and hear her sobs. God gave me the words, I know, because I couldn't have come up with them on my own. I replied, "You do love him, or you wouldn't be so hurt by him. When you love someone and they hurt you, you feel that. It hurts. He has serious problems we are trying to work out. We need to find out the right way to help him get better. But you need to remember, he loves you." In my mind, I knew and understood exactly what she was trying to express. To be honest, I was feeling similar emotions. If an adult grapples with it all, how can a young adolescent come to terms with it? We had all been hurt, bruised, disappointed, and driven to exhaustion by our circumstances. I've come to understand that, as much as we hated the situation, our son hated his own behavior and did not like himself for it. It was a destructive cycle.

Abby escaped to the safety of her own room. The family meeting didn't produce the results I was hoping for. But, as with so many other situations, I ended up discovering new insight into Ian. Later that evening, while getting ready for bed, Ian said, "She said she hates me, Mom. I heard her say it today." The core of the problem! He had overheard her, in her understandable frustration, saying she hated him. What I discovered that evening is that my son is very aware of the feelings of others. Beneath that tough-guy exterior exists a very sensitive little boy. Of course she didn't hate him, but she did hate the turmoil and state of anger our family was trapped in. For years she'd gone to her room, as violence and rage escalated outside of her door. The anguish these siblings endured was at times unbearable. And we were doing all we could to help Ian get better.

Because of his sensitivity coupled with defiance, Ian reacted to people that hurt him by lashing out and hurting them back either verbally, or in some instances, physically. Behavioral therapy alone was not enough to help him manage his anger. It only helped to a certain point. He needed the help of medication coupled with behavior modification. I know this was one of our darkest moments as a family. And I know families throughout this country, regardless of race, social status, or education, are experiencing this same darkness. It certainly was a dark moment for me as a mom. Which brings me to sibling relationships.

"Be My Valentine," by Ian, age 7
Poetry Contest Winner

The World of Siblings

The *Encyclopedia of Psychological Disorders: Sibling Rivalry,* says, "From our brothers and sisters, we learn how to communicate with others, behave socially, handle stress, negotiate for things we desire, express our feelings, and develop our thinking" (p.11). As the youngest of five children, I would certainly agree with that! While I experienced my share of sibling rivalry, I did indeed learn these things from my three sisters and my brother.

The book continues: "Siblings provide a child's first introduction to social parameters—how to fit in as well as how to stand up for oneself. Especially if children are close in age and if they interact as equals, their interaction can help them develop perspective about their place in the world, moral maturity, and competence in relating to other youngsters" (p.11). While this may be true for most children, those growing up with a challenging brother or sister oftentimes see things differently.

The following was retrieved from the website *Band-Aides and Blackboards.* This site is an excellent resource containing heartfelt comments for siblings, by siblings. Written about Don, this touching tribute captures the world of those growing up with challenging siblings:

Love Me, Love Me Not

The more I learn about sibling relationships, the more impressed I am with what "ambivalent" relationships they are—even when there is no disability. It seems that when disabilities are present, the ambivalence only gets stronger—the highs are higher (e.g. "Donny has brought me unending joy and laughter, and probably increased my sensitivity a hundred-fold." Would many of us make such a comment about a sibling who wasn't disabled?) and the lows are lower. (e.g. "On the other hand, sometimes I can't help but feel frustrated and cheated"). The challenge, I suppose, is to celebrate the insights

and sensitivity one gains as a result of the relationship, learn (sometimes painful) lessons from the
frustrations and then—somehow—move on.

I went on to read several accounts of siblings living with special
brothers and sisters. While some were written about children with
severe physical disabilities, many were written about developmental
problems as well. In any case, all the stories provided a window into
the hearts and souls of kids living with challenging siblings.

As with all children, the most important thing to keep open is
the line of communication. Parents need to be aware of the struggles
these siblings experience and never minimize them. I wanted to
show Abby, by modeling, the true meaning of a mother's love. By
doing this, I hoped to help her grow through the experiences into a
compassionate, loving person. Even when we feel there is nothing left
to give, we need to love these kids and encourage them in ways
unique to them. By doing this, each of our children will know there
is a place deep within our heart that belongs only to them.

When it Comes to Relatives and Friends....

As I've learned with my immediate family, it is important to let
our loved ones in. It took me years to feel comfortable with my own
family. Looking back, I don't know why I held on so tightly to that
image I had created. Perhaps I didn't want to appear a failure as a
mother. I had done such a great job with my daughter. Why couldn't
I have similar success with my son? Whatever the logic, it was irra-
tional. I now know that keeping my family at a distance cost me
dearly. I needed their love and support all along. I'm thankful I didn't
wait any longer to open up and share with them. It's important to give
family a chance to be just that—family. People who love and care for
you regardless of your situation.

Being a parent of a child with ODD, ADD, or ADHD, among
other disorders, can be exhausting. For the single parent, it can be
especially challenging. These special children test the limits of even

the best parents. When it's down to one parent as the primary care-giver, it is vital to take good care of yourself. You are not alone in this! Reach out and let others help you. Check into local parenting classes and support groups with parents in similar situations. Begin building a network for yourself and your family. Don't give in and don't give up.

I'm a firm believer in surrounding myself with positive people. As struggling parents, we are oftentimes fragile, easily discouraged, and lacking self-esteem. Being around negative individuals only brings us down. It's toxic to our mental and physical health. Again, we need support from positive, encouraging people. If a person doesn't support you, your parenting skills, or your family, move on. Don't waste time trying to change their opinion.

Regarding friends and neighbors, I think it's important to be honest with them, while practicing caution. Not everyone will be open-minded when it comes to child-rearing. Many individuals have a very black and white view of children. We know that oppositional defiance is anything but black and white. More like steel gray. The same is true for ADHD and similar disorders.

As parents and advocates for our children, we need to use good judgment when confiding in friends and neighbors. There is an art to knowing when to discuss our child and when not to. Feeling safe in a relationship takes time. Yet, developing close relationships with posi-tive individuals provides great support and comfort for us. It also helps our child. As I've learned when dealing with teachers, it's better to be honest about our child than to let others assume it's a bad atti-tude, intentional misbehavior, or unruliness. These kids have a real problem. Once a person realizes that, our kids have a better chance at being treated with understanding.

6
Blessed Are the Caregivers

As parents raising special kids, we need to realize our role as caregivers. I was familiar with the term "caregiver" and used it when referring to my mom. She has been a loving, devoted caregiver to my dad, who has been suffering with advanced Parkinson's disease. But me? A caregiver? It wasn't until I met with our family physician, Dr. Gene Carsia, that I started to view myself as just that.

Dr. Carsia, a family physician with fourteen years experience, has a private practice in Scottsdale, Arizona. His background includes a Bachelor of Science degree in behavioral neuroscience. While attending the University of Pittsburgh Medical School, Dr. Carsia conducted extensive research on improving antibiotics. He has always been interested in, and had a passion, for the development of new antibiotics to treat patients today. In addition, Dr. Carsia believes the new antidepressant medications are much improved from fifteen or twenty years ago. It was this progressive attitude that changed the direction of my life.

I was in Dr. Carsia's office to have Ian examined. It had been a rough, sleepless night, with Ian feeling shooting pain in his left ear. The numbing ear drops had helped, but not enough. Dr. Carsia confirmed Ian had an ear infection. After the exam he sent Ian out to the waiting room (under the supervision of the receptionist). It was then that he asked me how things were going. I opened up to him about the highly stressed home life we had been living for years. I asked his medical opinion on what we were experiencing with Ian.

At this point, we were under the care of our pediatrician and had stopped the behavioral therapy sessions. We were through with therapy for a while. We were seeking a medical solution for our desperate situation.

Dr. Carsia was attentive and compassionate as I gave a brief summary of the past several tumultuous years. As our physician, he had treated our family through the years for the usual sore throats and flu and had provided preventive care. I hadn't let Dr. Carsia in on our family situation. I was still protecting that perfect image. Looking back, I regret not confiding in him earlier. After discussing Ian, the conversation turned to me and my health.

It wasn't until I was depressed and exhausted that I sought help. I had withdrawn from social life and found myself sleeping to excess. I was working part-time as a substitute teacher. While this provided a healthy diversion, I began turning down more jobs than I took. It was just too hard to muster up the energy to face the day. My diet and exercise program had long gone by the wayside. I felt helpless and hopeless. The winter holidays were approaching, and I knew things would become even worse. I could actually feel the tension within regarding the upcoming season. Holidays and children who are oppositional can be a very difficult mix.

In addition, I didn't have much left emotionally to give to my teenage daughter, who needed me. I just felt empty and tired. Our marriage was suffering as a result of our not communicating. My son was setting us up against one another through manipulation and bullying. I was in the depths of despair. It was beginning to show.

After an exam and a conversation, Dr. Carsia diagnosed me as having "situational acute-brief depression." He explained that certain situations in life, for example, divorce, illness, and caring for a challenging child, can bring on depression and anxiety. Dr. Carsia said that caregivers, such as spouses of patients with Alzheimer's will oftentimes experience situational depression. In my case, I was not only feeling depressed I was also experiencing panic attacks. When we discussed this, Dr. Carsia helped calm my fears of losing my grip on reality. He assured me that what I was feeling—racing heart, sweaty palms, and panic—were all real physical reactions. He said, "The mind is very powerful. You can't turn it on and off like a light switch." It's just not that easy.

Dr. Carsia pointed out that all caregivers need support and, at times, treatment to help them "look forward and have hope." He prescribed an antidepressant medication for me to help with the depression and anxiety. In discussing the pros and cons of using medication to treat depression, Dr. Carsia shared an interesting story with me. He said, "With proper diagnosis and treatment, the use of medications has shown results beyond what I ever thought possible in medical school." He went on to say one of the most inspiring stories was of a patient who was showing signs of situational depression. "She was a teacher by profession. She was becoming unable to teach; the kids were annoying and frustrating her; she was considering leaving the field of education altogether. Within two weeks of treatment with an antidepressant medication, she was once again an effective, well-adjusted teacher." Dr. Carsia said that it was a "shocking" contrast to the woman who had been in his office two weeks earlier.

I believe that public awareness has increased regarding depression and the area of mental illness. Depression is real. People afflicted with depression need real help. So many Americans have been helped by proper diagnosis and medical treatment. "We aren't living in the 1800s anymore. Society has changed. People today face different challenges than those of the past. Effective medication is available today. Why not be open to more effective treatment for depression?" Dr. Carsia asks.

Dr. Carsia also pointed out that mental illness, including situational depression, crosses all economical, racial, and educational lines—just as do children struggling with oppositional defiance, ADHD, autism, and other disorders. Furthermore, the number of children being raised by grandparents today is staggering. These individuals are of a different generational era than today's parents; this difference brings both advantages and disadvantages to the table. While their experience and maturity are helpful in raising a child, their ideas on behavioral therapy and medication may differ from the ideas of today's younger generation.

While growing up, many of today's grandparents didn't discuss their private lives with others. Many viewed family problems as something to be hidden and dealt with privately. Therapy would not even have been a consideration. Today's grandparents may tend to hide their problems in raising a difficult child, leading to further frustration and despair. In addition to dealing with their own health issues and life changes, these grandparents, when dealing with difficult children, often find themselves depressed and unable to cope. At a time when their peers are entering retirement and the "golden years," these individuals are finding themselves raising another family. They don't know where to turn. Finding a compassionate doctor is the key to finding the right treatment.

In addition to generational differences, cultural differences also exist among parents. Parents may not effectively communicate to their physician because of beliefs that private struggles should be just that—private. In lower socioeconomic areas, children are less likely to get the proper diagnosis and needed treatment if the parents are not involved enough and don't communicate effectively with the physician. Parents truly must be their child's advocate. But they need to know where to begin, what questions to ask, and who to turn to.

As someone who has experienced it, depression is crippling. The days and nights all blur together in a dense fog. Panic attacks are real and frightening. Anxiety can overtake you. Simple tasks overwhelm you. Does a stigma still exist toward those individuals taking medication to treat depression? I believe it still does. Should it exist? Absolutely not. As Dr. Carsia stated, the physical changes in a person's body while experiencing anxiety, depression, and panic attacks are very real. There are excellent medications available today to help. Why would you resist that?

Dr. Carsia gave me precious gifts that afternoon. First, by taking the time to listen and empathize with me, he gave me the gift of compassion. He truly cared about me and my family. He wanted to see me get back on track and become effective in my role as a mother to my special son and participate in life again. If I wasn't effective, he explained, I wouldn't be able to handle the day-to-day demands I faced. I certainly agreed with that. The feeling of being overwhelmed constantly haunted me. I needed to step back, get myself the proper treatment, and begin to make better decisions.

Second, he gave me the gift of hope and a plan of action. I had hope that I would begin to feel better through treatment for depression. I'm so thankful that Dr. Carsia took the time to ask about my health. He reached out to me as a doctor and as a fellow human being. For that I'll be forever grateful.

7

Looking for a Miracle

The results from the neurological tests were sent to Dr. Trunzo. During our visit to discuss those results, Dr. Trunzo made a very helpful comparison. He looked at us and asked, "If your son had a hearing disorder and needed hearing aids, would you get them for him?" Of course, we replied that we would. How was this different?

I've often used that analogy about kids and medications. It tends to put things into perspective. We had exhausted all other avenues; we were now comfortable with treating Ian with medication. We discussed several different medications, their benefits and possible side effects. We all agreed to start off with a very low dose. We were proceeding with caution.

After years of doctors and therapists, we had a diagnosis for Ian's condition. We had a course of treatment which gave us hope for brighter days. Dr. Trunzo prescribed an antidepressant medication, an antiserotonin uptake inhibitor, in medical terms. He chose a to start treatment with a very low dose.

The purpose of using this medication was to help restore the balance of certain natural chemicals in the brain. The goal in treating Ian was to level off his extreme highs and lows and help him to be more balanced. Dr. Trunzo drew a diagram on the paper of the examining table as he explained the process. He drew two parallel lines about three inches apart, representing the emotional parameters of a normal person. He then drew a curving line sweeping back and forth, crossing the middle of that space. Some days, he explained, we all curve out of that space. For most, this would be a day in which we feel "off" or agitated. The goal is to stay somewhere in the middle of those parallel lines.

For Ian, his curving line was swinging wildly back and forth across that center. Our purpose in giving him this medication was to help guide him toward the middle and keep him balanced most of the time. Of course, like everyone, he would still have those "off" days. With success, he would feel less agitated and be better able to cope with his anxiety and frustration.

Dr. Trunzo advised us of possible side effects to watch for, which included nausea and diarrhea. We continued to take notes and felt confident with our decision. I felt a sense of relief that we were doing something—taking action to change the stressful pattern our family was locked into. We scheduled a follow-up visit and left the office with the prescription in hand and an angry boy following along.

Upon arriving home, Ian informed us that he was not going to take any medicine. Now here is a question for the doctors: How do you get an angry, defiant child to take a pill? Here is a mom's answer: Sneak it into ice cream! Devious? Dishonest? You bet, but it worked. Now, it didn't work right away. It took about ten days to see the positive effect of the medication. Those were a rough ten days. I called Dr. Trunzo and asked for advice; he was very supportive and patient. He suggested giving the drug in liquid form, and that brought back some vivid memories.

In my mind I was taken back to a time when Ian was four years old and in the emergency room with an ear infection. We found ourselves taking him in after midnight when he awoke and began screaming. He was in such pain. It had come on suddenly and without warning, like most childhood ear infections do. After diagnosing an infection, the doctor wanted Ian on an antibiotic immediately. While the nurse began administering an orange-flavored medication to Ian, he sat bolt upright and spit sticky orange liquid all over my husband, the nurse, and me. I can still see it: the four-year-old, exhausted, red-faced boy projecting orange syrup in a rapid-fire action as we all stood by. It was not a pleasant experience but like so many other episodes, rather humorous in hindsight.

I knew that, somehow, I had to get this medication into Ian's system in order for him to get the positive effects. It just wouldn't be in liquid form. Desperate times call for desperate measures, hence the ice cream trick. It worked. I would recommend it in the early days of medicating defiant children. It wasn't long until Ian was calmer, more reasonable, and compliant when it was time to take the medication. I believe he knew how much better it made him feel. He wasn't about to admit that to me though. Not yet.

By the time we started the medication, we were cautiously optimistic. We watched for possible side effects including nausea, trouble sleeping, dry mouth, dizziness, and weight loss. We were most concerned about a possible loss of appetite. Our son was on the thin side, and we didn't want to see a significant weight loss. After fifteen weeks, we increased the dosage slightly and were confident that side effects were minimal; weight loss was not an issue. He did, however, have trouble falling asleep at night. This had never been a problem before. So, he fell asleep later in the evening, but the daytime hours were much more manageable for all of us.

We were amazed and grateful at the change in his personality. It did not take weeks, as in many cases, to see the therapeutic effects. The change was fast and obvious. He was not as angry but he was still edgy and easily frustrated. Yet, each day seemed to be slightly better than the last. It couldn't have gotten much worse than it had been.

Although Dr. Trunzo doesn't like to refer to any one medication as a "miracle pill," I viewed it as such simply because it had an incredibly positive effect on my son. It just smoothed out the edges. He was calmer and more at peace. This is what Dr. Trunzo had referred to during our initial visit: giving our son relief through low-dose medication and helping the dynamics of the entire family.

It was indeed helping our entire family. The difference was obvious. Oh, we were still battle weary, but the intensity of it seemed to have dropped a bit. After so many years of hurt and disappointment, I wasn't quite ready to open my heart to Ian again. I was still guarding my spirit from defiant attacks. I knew this wasn't a cure and that it would be a process, but we were on the road to healing.

8

Lost in San Francisco

It was because of this hope and progress that Roger and I decided to attend my only brother's wedding in San Francisco. Because I love John very much, I desperately wanted to be present. It would take place two weeks after we had begun the medical treatment. We discussed our concerns with Dr. Trunzo. Would it be better if we didn't go? Would Ian be okay with a family friend babysitting at our home? It would be only three days. We would plan activities, stock the refrigerator, leave our family car for outings, and make sure Abby, Ian, and the babysitter were safe and well taken care of.

Dr. Trunzo felt it would be very healthy for the two of us to have some respite time. He encouraged us and even gave us his cell phone number to call if we needed him. As I've said, this is a compassionate man, dedicated to children and families. After discussing it with the doctor, each other, our children, and the babysitter, Roger and I decided to take the opportunity to be part of the magical weekend in San Francisco. With trepidation, I booked our flight. We would arrive Thursday and stay until Sunday afternoon. We would have one evening and three full days in San Francisco.

I viewed this as a wonderful opportunity to be a guest at John and Ali's wedding on the beautiful grounds of the Presidio Park, located on the northern point of the San Francisco peninsula. I had visions of the viewing the majestic Golden Gate Bridge, touring wine country, and enjoying seafood at fine restaurants with my husband. It was a chance for us as a couple to be just that—a couple. Time to enjoy conversation and each other. Three days of cable cars, walking,

75

touring, and celebrating a beautiful wedding. That was the plan. But of course not all plans go accordingly.

A Golden Day

I started off the weekend with such hope in my heart! Hope for Roger and me to reconnect as a couple, enjoy uninterrupted conversation, and forget about all the tension for at least three days. What better place to do just that? I soon discovered that, just as I had moved my family 2,000 miles across the country and brought all our problems with us, Roger and I also brought our problems with us to San Francisco. Our relationship had lasted through many violent storms, but we were indeed weary, weather-beaten survivors. One weekend away, even in one of the most beautiful cities in the world, wasn't going to bring our relationship back that quickly. In fact, I've learned that parents of special children must redefine their marriage throughout the years. Life changes you. It changes your marriage. Changing, growing, and communicating in a marriage is not an option if that marriage is going to last.

We arrived Thursday afternoon and met our family and friends in our hotel lobby. The next day, Friday, would be spent any way we wished in the city at the Golden Gate. Some of the guests were planning a day seeing the sights—the Golden Gate Bridge, Chinatown, and Fisherman's Wharf to name a few. On Saturday we would be at the Presidio watching John and Ali exchange wedding vows.

Roger and I had our handy *Baedeker's San Francisco Map and Guide* to help us navigate the beautiful city. Thursday, after visiting with my brother, sisters, and friends, Roger and I walked over to a nearby pier and strolled hand-in-hand, enjoying the moment. We were able to join a group heading out to the bay on a large tour boat.

This tour offered us a great way to see Alcatraz Island and the Golden Gate Bridge. The hour-long excursion cruised by the former Alcatraz Penitentiary then along the bay past the Golden Gate Bridge. We laughed, took pictures, and enjoyed our fellow passengers as we took in the sights. After docking, we walked back to Scoma's

Restaurant on Pier 47 and enjoyed that seafood dinner we had been looking forward to. Everything was right with the world. The sunset was gorgeous, the weather was perfect, with a gentle breeze, and three entire days in San Francisco were ahead of us.

The First Phone Call Home

When we returned to our hotel room, we called home to check in. With a prayer in my heart and holding my breath, I talked to Abby first. She sounded good and assured me everything was going well. I then talked with Ian, who sounded calm and happy. Our babysitter, always perky, sounded just fine. Maybe this would be okay after all.

The next morning, we awoke looking forward to a free day in the city. What should we do? We began by taking a walk to Ghirardelli Square, not far down the street from our hotel. There, amongst art galleries, gardens, fountains, and terraces, we sipped fresh coffee and even indulged in some famous Ghirardelli chocolates.

While there, we talked about renting a car and driving up to California's Napa and Sonoma Valleys. In addition to our guide book, we had also brought along a beautiful book, *Wine Country*, by John Doerper. We were able to map out our trip, which included visiting a few wineries and enjoying the fine art of wine tasting. We headed back to prepare for our trip. However, the weekend was about to take a U-turn.

The Dreaded Blinking Light

Upon returning to our room, we noticed the message light blinking on our phone. I knew. Call it "mother's instinct," if you wish. I just knew things weren't going well at home. The call confirmed it. Our sitter was having trouble getting Ian to cooperate. While Abby was fine, Ian was being quite difficult. He had been taking his medication regularly. He was eating. He was safe. He just was being a real stinker. I gave her some tips on defusing the situation and talked with Abby also. I then talked with Ian and hung up feeling hopeful that things would settle down. They didn't.

We went ahead with our trip to wine country but it was stressful. That phone call had taken the glow off everything. The burden of worry we were both carrying was clouding over this beautiful day along the winding roads. Still, we persevered with hope and prayer. If there's one thing we've learned, it's to enjoy the moment. Easier said than done, however. We did our best.

Returning that evening, the two of us were quiet and tired, from the combination of the day's activities and the worry. I lay my head down, hoping to get through my brother's wedding the next day. If we had to cut the trip short, we would leave just after the wedding. It wasn't looking good. I tried to keep my tight grip on the hope for a good weekend with Roger, but it felt like someone had greased up my hands.

The next morning I called home to check in. While things weren't great, our sitter and Abby assured us they were okay and asked us not to come home early. They didn't want us to miss the wedding. I was beginning to realize that there were better alternatives to this weekend, which I should have considered. We could have brought Abby and Ian with us. In my desperate attempt to reconnect with Roger and have time away, I had missed the opportunity to bring our children to San Francisco. Although traveling with Ian had never been easy, this weekend was turning out to be not so easy either. If I had it to do over again, I would have either brought our children with us or declined the invitation. As it turned out, John and Ali picked up on our tension and stress. We weren't hiding much from anyone anymore.

A Peaceful Little Chapel on the Bay

Once again I felt disconnected, as if I were watching scenes from my life as they occurred. Going through the motions. Here we were in a beautiful historic church filled with wooden pews, hardwood floors, stained-glass windows. The scent from the flowers, lilies and roses, filled the air. I watched my brother, with love in his eyes, and his bride, with her beautiful glow, exchange vows as they started a new life together. I found myself reflecting on our lives and my feelings of despair became more poignant. So many mixed emotions.

Following the ceremony there was a photo shoot on the gorgeous grounds of the Presidio. What a romantic, beautiful setting! Afterward, our intimate group enjoyed dinner at A. Sabella's Restaurant, overlooking the stunning views of downtown San Francisco. After the dinner reception and several heartfelt toasts to the newlyweds, we continued the celebration. The magical night wasn't over yet.

We took our celebration to Harry Denton's Starlight Room located at the top of the Drake Hotel, overlooking Union Square and Macy's. There, we danced to live music and looked out at the twinkling lights of beautiful San Francisco. Again, the feeling of watching life happen from a distance.

9

Finding a Way in the Desert

It was during this weekend that I really began to open up to my sister Kathy. I couldn't keep it all inside any longer. Besides, being the big sister, she was in tune with me and knew things were terribly wrong. We were able to share some quiet moments Saturday night, in the comfort of the large, inviting lobby. There, in oversized, comfy chairs, we shared conversation and tears. I began to tell the story of our journey—from the beginning.

The realization hit me. All these years, I had kept my siblings and parents out of my own family's lives when it came to our problems. Then I would be upset that they didn't understand why I was tired or frustrated. How could they? I had done such an excellent job of keeping up the façade, they had no idea how our family really was. I had three sisters and a brother who would do anything for me. Now I had a sister-in-law, too, along with two great brothers-in-law. Instead of reaching out, I had shut them out. What a shame. Here I was with a big, loving family, and I didn't let them help me. I've learned so much through this journey. One of the main lessons was how incredibly important family is and how very blessed I am to have them.

On this day, before we left for home, Kathy and I laughed, cried, and prayed together. I view this day as both the darkest day and the turning point of my life. I couldn't continue without help from my family. I wasn't even sure I could continue at all until I talked and prayed with Kathy. She gave me hope that I wasn't carrying the burden alone. Facing my return home, I became overwhelmed with emotion. Now that I had let my sister in, we were both returning to our homes on opposite ends of the country.

Her husband, John, said good-bye and went to get the shuttle van that would take them to the airport. As Kath and I said good-bye, I felt as if I were hanging onto a life ring in a raging sea. I just wanted her to take over for me. I wanted to just to turn it over and say, would you please? But of course, I couldn't do that. Instead, I realized that I had to hand it over to God. While that was a comforting thought, it didn't make Kathy's departure any easier. We stood and hugged each other as John entered the lobby. Their van was ready.

Be strong, I told myself. Hang on. You've done it this long, you'll be fine. We hugged again, and it felt so good as Kath held me in her arms. I felt loved and protected. I didn't want to let go. But I had to.

As I watched Kath leave through the big glass doors, I was about five years old again. I was scared, tired, and broken. I was aware of people walking past me as I stood with my arms folded in front of me, silent tears streaming down my cheeks. About three minutes passed; then I saw Kathy, tears down her cheeks also, come back through those doors. She grabbed me in her arms and hugged me so tightly. I still cry when I recall this moment. Talk about love for your sister. How could I possibly have missed this for so long? I knew I would never be far from my family's loving reach again.

Finding the Good

We returned home to one very tired-out babysitter. Abby had, as usual, risen to the occasion and helped to keep things going in our absence. Ian was healthy and safe. I learned many valuable lessons over that weekend. If we had taken the kids with us, would it have been better? I don't know. I do know that the time I had with my sister has changed my life. And my brother and sister-in-law? Living happily ever after.

A Way in the Desert

Not long after my return home from San Francisco, Kathy sent me an encouraging card with this verse written in it, from Isaiah 43:18-19: "Forget the former things; do not dwell on the past. See, I am doing a new thing! Now it springs up; do you not perceive it? I am making a way in the desert and streams in the wasteland." This verse spoke to me. I had been living (literally) in the Southwest desert and (spiritually) in a wasteland. I was in such a dark place, consumed by my circumstances. I was about to discover that all the challenges and trials I had been experiencing were shaping me into the woman God intended me to be. I believe He works everything out for good. I had no idea of the miracles and joy that were to come.

10

Shared Stories

I was in the hallway of the neighborhood community center, waiting to pick up Ian from summer sports camp. As I was looking at some creative artwork I heard the voice. The voice of desperation that says, "I know where this situation is going, please let it stop." I looked to my right and saw a boy about nine years old swinging a backpack back and forth. He looked angry and stubborn: defiance. He stood behind a large pillar in the hallway. Also to my right, near the exit door, was a woman in her early 40s, dressed in business attire. She looked frustrated and very tired. Wandering around nearby was another boy, the other sibling. He seemed pretty calm. I soon discovered that both boys had serious problems.

Her voice was pleading, "Nick, let's go. We need to go now." He refused again and again, and I could feel the tension in the air thickening. She then walked to the office, where the door was closed, and asked the desk attendant, "Is Bob in?" Bob, the director of the camp, is calm, confident, and in control. He also has a contagious smile and is a great communicator to parents and kids alike.

At this point, I made myself unobtrusive and looked at the artwork made by summer campers. I knew what this woman was going through and I didn't want to add to her burden by watching the episode progress. I've learned that the response and judgment by others simply adds to the desperation I'm feeling at the time. In fact, as I've learned, the reactions and harsh judgment of onlookers is one of the single most harmful aspects of this whole struggle. It causes much anguish on the parent's or guardian's part and only compounds the problem.

So, while appearing not to notice, I heard Bob approach and ask calmly, "What's up?" The woman explained that her son was refusing to leave with her and said, "I need your help." As she choked out these words, my heart reached out to her and I said a prayer for her. "Please, God, be with this woman right now. Bless her heart with a small ray of hope which will grow into a heart full of hope. Please be with her and her son. Let the Holy Spirit change his heart." I believe in the power of prayer. I also believe God works through us to help others in need.

It took a full twelve minutes in that hallway for Bob and the mom to get Nick to leave on his own accord. At ten years old and about ninety-five pounds, picking him up forcibly and leaving with him was not a realistic option.

Bob handled the situation calmly as he tried to defuse the situation. He talked with the boy, saying that this was his mom, and that when she was at camp, she was the boss. He needed to listen to her and do as she asked. Somehow Bob reached the boy and he decided to cooperate and leave with his mother. Later, I discovered that the woman not only had one son with defiant behavior but two.

As I collected Ian, whom I am so thankful for and look at with new eyes, I reflected on what had just taken place. My thoughts were with that special woman and her son. I know that the struggle continued and most likely escalated again in the car as she went home with her children.

I wondered to myself, how much Bob truly understood what they were dealing with. It caused me to look deeper into his knowledge of ODD and other disorders that many campers struggle with. I went on to discover that the camp provided all employees with training courses which address various behavioral and physical disorders. These staff leaders and youth volunteers are educated on various disorders such as physical disorders, learning disorders, ADD, ADHD, and ODD.

In addition, I learned that the city of Scottsdale offers adapted recreation services geared for persons of all ages who have various disabilities. In this program, children with special needs are main-streamed (included) in the after-school and summer programs. Upon visiting the city's website, I also discovered that participation in Special Olympics, outdoor retreats, and community integration services are also offered.

I learned the importance of knowing not only the discipline procedures but the training and education of staff members working with our children. It's important to thoroughly investigate the programs we enroll our children in. We must know if the individuals working with our kids are able to nurture, cope with, and encourage them throughout their day's activities. It's all a piece of the same puzzle, part of the support system we need to build for our children and our families.

Which brings me back to the woman struggling with her son. What does her network of support look like? Does she even have support? Does she have a diagnosis for her sons? Does she have medical coverage to take advantage of health care options? Does she even know about the help that is available, or is she buying into the claim that her boys simply are "being boys?" So many parents accept this defiance as simply behavioral when in fact other biological disorders may exist, compounding the problem.

In our case, we spent years in search of those solutions, and we were fortunate to have the resources to seek help. ODD affects children regardless of their economic position. It is a tricky condition which all the money in the world won't help unless you find the right solution. It may be a combination of solutions: behavioral therapy, medical treatment, respite care, and support groups. Whatever solution we find, we can count on one thing: it will be changing again as the child grows and changes. The good news is that, once we have some positive course of action, we are better equipped to handle those changes and stay the course. It all comes down to hope.

Special People

It's a funny thing, this ODD mom stuff. You never know when someone will share her experiences with you regarding her own children, all the while not knowing that you've got your own set of very real problems. In some cases, the problems a person is dealing with are exactly what you're experiencing. You think to yourself, "If only she knew." This happened to me quite often and I really listened to what people were sharing. I wondered how it felt to open up and honestly discuss the struggles. It was comforting to know that I wasn't alone in the challenges I was facing but not comforting enough yet for me to feel safe to discuss my own child. That wall took years to build, and I realized it would take considerable time and effort to tear it down. But I was beginning to do just that, brick by brick.

Michael

I was working at my church preparing meals for our teen youth program when a fellow volunteer opened her heart to me. We were arranging tables and chairs, meals, and refreshments. Jane started off by talking about her son Michael, who was fifteen years old. Her first comment that jumped out at me was, "My son is the kind of kid you just can't say 'no' to. Really! You cannot say 'no;' he just does not listen. You wouldn't believe it!" Oh, yes I would.

I do, in fact, believe it completely. I have lived it for years. Jane went on to say that she and her husband had been married thirty-four years, and at times she does not know how they survived it all. This term "survived" is quite appropriate. *Merriam-Webster's Collegiate Dictionary* defines survive as "to remain alive or in existence; to live on; to continue to function or prosper despite; to withstand."

How many of us have said at the end of an exhausting day with our child, "I don't know how long I can survive this"? That may sound dramatic to some who haven't lived it, but I literally had days in which it was all I could do to "continue to function or prosper despite" the oppositional defiant grip on my son.

The Dance of Defiance

From an early age her son had been very bright and very defiant. As she stated, the word "no" meant nothing to him. She also used the term "demanding" in our conversation. Does that sound familiar? I know that from the moment of birth Ian was very demanding. He urgently needed to be fed, and he let everyone know from his screeching cries that he was not happy to have been disturbed. From that moment the demands became clear and the tumultuous journey began.

I hadn't known Jane long, but I did notice she appeared to struggle with serious health problems. That evening I learned part of the reason why. She admitted then that raising Michael had taken a serious toll on her health as well as on her marriage. In discussing their struggles, she went on to discuss their time spent living in another country. For two years she and her family had lived in a foreign land as part of her husband's career path. When asked how Michael did with that change, Jane said while it was hard to be away from the United States, it was a healthy diversion for her own life. It gave her a focus besides her son. She studied the language and culture of her temporary new home. It was a time of personal growth for her.

We went on to discuss how Michael had been on Ritalin for ADHD since he was two years old. When I asked her if they'd considered any of the newer medications available, she said she really hadn't. In fact, she looked rather surprised at the idea of changing medications. I understood this because once we finally get to a better place for Ian, we don't want to mess with the formula! Unfortunately, though, a child grows and experiences hormonal changes. Medications must be closely monitored and periodically changed. Eventually, we need to address a change in dosage and must continue to seek the best treatment options. In this case, she felt her son was growing normally, progressing in school, and overall doing well on Ritalin. Except he continued to be a child struggling with ADHD, who was now in a man-sized body.

Dr. James Dobson, in his book, *The New Strong-Willed Child*, discusses ADHD and treatment options with Dr. Walt Larimore:

One problem with some of the older ADHD medications was that their effects didn't last more than a few hours at most. This meant that extra doses would have to be given at school or later in the afternoon once the child was home. Worse yet, when the short-acting medications wore off, a rebound effect sometimes occurred, during which the child's symptoms and behaviors actually worsened! (p.196)

Dr. Larimore continues to discuss newer medications available for children and families. He points out that "the treatment for ADHD should be individualized and tailored for each child and each family. So, while there is no 'best' course of treatment there are a number of excellent options." (p. 196)

As with any other disorder, medical treatments need to be carefully considered on a case-by-case basis. What works well for one child may not work for another. I've learned to read as much as I can, ask countless questions, and take notes as Ian tries a new medication. Again, we are our kids' advocates in all respects.

In our conversation, Jane assumed that I was speaking from my experiences in the classroom. She couldn't possibly have known that my polite little boy, who had helped serve last Sunday's teen meals, struggled with such defiance. I had worked so hard to portray the perfect family, I succeeded in building a brick wall around us. It was a very attractive red, but a brick wall nonetheless. What I truly had succeeded in was isolating my family.

To add to this story, I am ashamed to admit that I had been guilty of judging Michael during the year. Proceeding through the buffet line, he was always quick to point out what he didn't like about the dinner provided. He rarely smiled and was quite abrasive. He was abrupt with the volunteers and had an arrogance that people were quick to notice. Once my conversation started with Jane that evening, I realized Michael had special challenges that reached far beyond mere rudeness. Worse than that knowledge was the realization that I had made the mistake so many others make: I had judged

Michael based on outward appearances only. I had no idea of the struggles he and his family had been living.

All along I'd been struggling with my own son, and here I was judging someone else. Even with being as aware as I thought I was, I fell into that trap. This proves that we truly do not know what some people are living. The kid in the grocery store who screams uncontrollably in a rage; the girl who refuses to walk with her mom down the sidewalk; the toddler who arches his back, red faced and screaming, as his young dad tries to pick him up—these people are living in despair. As Henry David Thoreau said in 1854, "The mass of men lead lives of quiet desperation." This rings true today for many parents struggling with challenging children. Even once they disclose their struggles, we do not know what their days hold until we've lived them ourselves.

Looking at Jane and opening my heart to her words and emotions, I could see the experience of it in her eyes. She had been living in survival mode, trying to hang on day by day and do the best she could. Not only was she isolated by circumstances, she was in another country during some of that time. Her honesty in admitting the hardship on her marriage and her health caused by raising a difficult child rang so true with me. The evening wasn't over yet, however. Another special woman had a story to share.

Jason

In contrast to my friend Jane, Linda had a similar story with a different approach: humor. Always one with a smile and a small, sweet voice, Linda opened her heart to share her trials and tribulations in raising her fifteen-year-old son, Jason. He was diagnosed during early elementary school with ADHD. Where Jane's burden was heavy and had taken an obvious toll on her health, marriage, and outlook, Linda's burden, while similar in nature, was approached with resiliency and a keen sense of humor. I was struck by the difference in their coping mechanisms. It gave me insight as to how each of us is unique in the way we handle adversity.

Linda explained that she was the mom at Parent Night looking into the option of community colleges rather than universities. While many parents were asking the counselors about scholarships and Ivy League colleges, Linda wanted to know about other options for our kids. I happened to be at that meeting and was encouraged and proud of her as she raised her hand and asked about alternatives to the university track. Later, she discussed her dismay that our community acts as if every child is destined to go on to a university. She was realistic with her expectations and hope for her son. "At this point," she said, "our goal is to see Jason graduate from high school." Given up? No. Realistic? Yes. She wanted to set realistic goals for her son to insure his success. Not every student is destined to go on to a four-year university. Trade schools, community colleges, and on-the-job training may be more appropriate options for some kids. Exploring all the options is the key.

Linda with the sweet voice and smile is her son's best advocate, and she does it with a healthy dose of humor. I've learned a lot from her.

Matthew

Sarah's story struck a familiar chord within my heart. Her seven-year-old son, Matthew, had been recently diagnosed with obsessive compulsive disorder (OCD). As with many children, Matthew had coexisting conditions. He was also struggling with ODD and learning challenges. Sarah's story touched my heart because I had lived it. Through a series of heartfelt emails I could feel the struggle and pain Sarah was in. She had been on a seven-year journey of her own and was reaching out to me. Like me, she was fiercely protective of her son, having experienced harsh judgments and unfounded criticism from individuals who did not understand.

During our initial conversations, Sarah shared that the hardest thing for her, personally, had been experiencing rejection and isolation. She didn't know any other mom in her situation. I've discovered many moms in our situation; that very same isolation had kept us all apart from one another. For Sarah, it had caused rifts in relationships with friends and family over the past five years. When I first met her, Sarah had turned the corner on being concerned about how others viewed her and Matthew. With a background in public relations, Sarah realized she had been overly concerned with image. She was in the process of letting that go. Like me, Sarah was beginning to let others in who might lend much-needed support.

After several pediatricians, social workers, psychiatrists, parenting classes, and even a sensory integration clinic, a neurologist gave them the diagnosis which Sarah was so grateful for. Like so many parents, Sarah and her husband needed to have name for what they were facing. They knew something was wrong. It had a name. Now they could move forward.

What disturbed me the most about Sarah's story was the conflicting responses she had received from pediatricians she visited. One referred to medications as "plastic surgery for the brain" while another was quick to write a prescription on the spot without in-depth testing. At least one pediatrician admitted a lack of knowledge about Matthew's condition and referred Sarah to a psychiatrist. This roller coaster of conflicting advice puts parents, already confused and searching, into further despair. As Sarah explained, "My biggest worry was that I'd medicate him prematurely and unnecessarily, or that I would be causing him harm by not medicating and thus helping him cope." Most experts agreed, however, that good counseling should be exhausted first. Finding "good" counseling, especially for children with OCD and ODD, oftentimes presents a challenge. Finding the underlying causes and treating them appropriately gets to the root of the defiant behavior. Unfortunately, the road is strewn with boulders and riddled with pitfalls for parents and families.

Continuing to search for answers and treatment, Sarah had been in close contact with Matthew's school. His teachers repeatedly told her that he was performing well and was a "model citizen." They went on to say that, while they saw some anxiety, it was nothing out of the ordinary. Sarah admitted that, for the past two years, the school had suggested that perhaps she was the one with anxiety and should relax about her child.

This brings me back to one diagnostic feature of oppositional defiant disorder. As stated in the *DSM-IV-TR*, "Manifestations of the disorder are almost invariably present in the home setting, but may not be evident at school or in the community." Matthew had been a textbook example of showing a pattern of defiant behaviors at home while being a model citizen at school, leading to total frustration for his parents and family. The school was questioning Sarah's parenting, even going so far as to suggest it was she who was anxious!

Sarah tried to explain the emotional struggle she experiences when her son becomes frustrated and at times even begs for help. She described it also as a spiritual battle, and she has stepped up her prayer life. As do so many other children with ODD, Matthew has a very hard time with special occasions. During his brother's birthday party Matthew became violent, threatening to hurt himself with a knife. Knowing how out of bounds this behavior was brought Sarah and her husband back to the professionals. It was then that they received their diagnosis; they received a name for what they were dealing with, obsessive-compulsive disorder, oppositional defiant disorder, and learning challenges. They've been reassured by doctors that, with the right intervention and understanding, Matthew has every opportunity to lead a fulfilling and successful life. That reassurance is wonderful, but without a course of action, parents are left to their own devices. As Sarah stated, they have a diagnosis but no one to help with a follow-up plan. They have been referred to a behavioral pediatrician and are hoping to gain a better understanding of medications and, if needed, a referral to a behavioral therapist. Still feeling the weight of the decision to use medications, Sarah is continuing to search for answers.

Matthew is fortunate to have two involved parents who are dedicated advocates on his behalf. They are partners in parenting their child through faith and determination and are facing each new day with hope. Disorders like OCD and ODD put a strain on the strongest of families. Even with the best medical insurance and resources, parents of a special child are often at a loss when dealing with professionals, educators, friends, families, and neighbors when it comes to their special child. This challenging role gives meaning to the ancient American Indian saying, "Never judge a man until you've walked a mile in his moccasins."

11

A Six-Month
Roller Coaster Ride

Ian was now seven years old and his tantrums were at their peak. It wasn't long after our return from San Francisco that it seemed the medication was no longer as effective. Ian was physically aggressive toward me and becoming that way with Abby and Roger. He did not fear or respect us. The dinner hour was extremely stressful. If he was unhappy with a meal or any detail, we knew that the dinner hour was over. He began tipping chairs over as he stormed to his room. All along the way, he would pound his fist against the walls.

He would verbally threaten us and scream that he hated his family. This was a daily occurrence. I went to bed each night exhausted, fearful, and resentful. Most of his anger was aimed at me, and I was primarily responsible for the disciplining. I struggled with Roger's apparent lack of response; as a gentle person, taking the role of disciplinarian was difficult for him. He was raised an only child in a quiet, relaxed, and loving family. His late father continues to be the gentlest human being I've ever met. His mother had a joy and love of life unmatched by most.

On the other hand, I grew up in a noisy, loving household of seven, the youngest child of a spirited Irish and Scottish mom and a dedicated Italian dad. We were raised in the Catholic faith, surrounded by love, good food, and laughter. I both feared and respected my parents. One cross look from Mom or Dad was all it took to change my behavior. Along with this respect, I also held deep love and admiration toward them. I still do.

In my own household as an adult woman, I felt as if no one was sticking up for me. Our home wasn't filled with love and laughter; it was filled with tension and unhappiness. I felt alone and left to deal with everything myself. I wanted my children to have the same respect and love toward us that I had had toward my own parents. I realized that I was my own person and my husband, his own person. Yes, our children need to respect us but it has to be within our own unique family dynamics. We had to create the structure our son and daughter so desperately needed. Each with our own style and personality, we had to command respect within the family we had created. It would take prayer, determination, the right treatment, and support from others to make that a reality.

Looking back, I realize Roger was at a loss about how to handle Ian. Roger was struggling with his own fears and isolation. He did not know what to do; at times he stepped away. Always a good provider and committed to our family, he threw himself into his work, home responsibilities, and daily tasks. It was what he knew. He was exhausted as well. He let Ian rage and, like the rest of us, hoped the rage would soon end. Abby spent many hours in her room, trapped in our dysfunctional family. We did not go out to dinner. We did not go to the movies, the park, a ballgame, or any other social activity. I had given up trying to look like the perfect family. We were not. On one occasion, I simply sat outside and rocked quietly on a glider until my husband came home. It had been a difficult afternoon, full of tantrums. It didn't matter who saw me sitting there. I must have looked battle weary. I was. It was the first time I really didn't care what others thought. I look back on that moment as a sort of enlightenment for me. It was freeing to let go of the image I had fiercely held onto. That had taken up so much energy, that I no longer had.

We were living with the knowledge that at any moment Ian could explode. We were physically and emotionally tired after living with years of struggles and unrest; we couldn't do it much longer. I started dwelling on lost dreams and lost years. I would describe this part of the journey as the depths of despair.

12

Bumps in the Road

Overall, things were going well with Ian's treatment until he had a bad headache one Friday evening. I gave him Children's Motrin, as I had in the past, and he went to bed. The next day he was itchy and asked me to scratch his back. I noticed red bumps on his belly and back. They were spreading to his arms. I was concerned; I watched it and we gave it another day. What followed was a weekend I never want to experience again.

I called Dr. Trunzo and asked if this could be a reaction to the medication. He hadn't seen this type of reaction in any of his other patients who were on this medication. Since Ian had been taking it for some time, he did not believe it was a reaction to it. I pulled the Children's Motrin bottle off the shelf and read the following printed on its label: "Allergy alert: Ibuprofen may cause a severe allergic reaction which may include hives, facial swelling, asthma (wheezing), and shock." I discussed this with Dr. Trunzo, and he agreed that it could be a reaction to the Motrin. Although I had given ibuprofen to Ian in the past, this could be a reaction to it. Dr. Trunzo advised me to immediately stop any ibuprofen products and suggested giving Ian Benadryl Allergy to counter the allergic reaction.

Part Mom, Part Pharmacist

Along with the Benadryl, I bought Aveeno Oatmeal Bath so Ian could get some relief. His discomfort was increasing by the minute. He was miserable. By now he was covered head to toe with red welts.

I couldn't comfort him. He was begging me to "do something!" He stayed home from school Monday, Tuesday, and Wednesday. The only way I could comfort him was to keep him in a cool bath.

I reached Dr. Trunzo late in the evening on his cell phone. I wanted to avoid a trip to the emergency room, knowing it could be an all-night event. Ian wanted to be home in the cool baths. Dr. Trunzo advised that the emergency room doctor would most likely give him an injection of steroids to combat the reaction. The doctor and I agreed that this reaction was being compounded by the Benadryl. He was having a reaction to that as well.

I stopped the Benadryl immediately, kept Ian in lukewarm Aveeno baths, sang to him, read to him, comforted him, and prayed. He eventually slept on and off. By Thursday, he was feeling better.

Through this experience, I discovered the adverse effects antihistamines can have on individuals. This includes excitability, especially in children. We were about to learn how the adverse effects impacted our son.

Behavioral Spikes

While Ian was recovering from his severe reaction to ibuprofen and then the antihistamine, his personality began to change. He became violent and enraged, as he had done before the treatment with medication began. However, there was a deviant twist to it. Admittedly, it had been a very traumatic week for him; he had physically been through a lot. Now he was angry, easily agitated, and frustrated.

After one particular episode, I sent him to his room to cool off. He was quiet and I hoped he had fallen asleep for much-needed rest. Such wasn't the case. A little later that evening, when tucking him into bed, I noticed he had pulled his comforter over the sides of his bunk-bed railing. When I pulled it back, I saw that he had somehow carved deep lines into the light cherry wood. Along the side he had even carved his name. I was shocked! He took such pride in his bedroom set. How could he do this? Why? He was sheepish and remorseful. The explanation that followed, however, chilled my heart.

The Devil Made Me Do It

In his own words, Ian explained, "The voice in my head made me do it. I feel this voice, Mom. It starts in my feet and moves up into my stomach then into my head." He was scared; I was scared. Could this be an altered state, resulting from the antihistamines I had given him to stop the allergic reaction? My heart went out to my son. Shaking, I held him and prayed.

Beyond Mischievous

There was more to come. The very next day we heard a knock on our front door. Our neighbors, who were selling their home, had a situation. Someone had removed the "For Sale" sign from their front yard. Did we have any idea what had happened to it? Ian and the neighbor's children were running around the neighborhood in search of this sign. Ian came back in and made a confession. He had taken the sign out of the hard desert ground, run across the desert, and thrown it over a six-foot fence toward a canal. A pretty big feat for a seven-year-old boy!

I saw the protective bubble I had so diligently placed around my son and our family pop into thin air. The neighbors now must consider him a real troublemaker. As concerned parents, we believed the right thing to do was have him take responsibility for his actions and walk over to the neighbors' house and tell the truth. There was only one problem: he was defiant. He had no intention of doing that. The best we could do was have him walk along with my husband and ring their doorbell. My husband did the talking while Ian stood next to him. Not the way I wanted it to go, but I believe the lesson was learned. Under the circumstances, I was grateful he went on his own accord. In the past it would have been a physical challenge to get him over there.

After a day or so, Roger and I talked to our neighbors and briefly explained the hives, the reaction to the antihistamine, and his distress. All the while as I heard myself talking, I sounded hollow and full of excuses. Even though it was the truth, there was so much more behind it. I felt they had already made their judgment and I wasn't going to change it. They were gracious and kind, yet I knew they had their doubts. This goes back to that isolation we parents feel in trying to get along with others while experiencing the effects of a challenging child.

The sign was restored. The relationship with our neighbors was not. They moved away a year later.

13
The End of the Road

It was about this time in Ian's life that he began giving me a look. The best name for it was "a look of contempt." *Merriam-Webster's Collegiate Dictionary* defines contempt as "the act of despising; lack of respect or reverence for something." Yes, that described the look and the message I was receiving. Contempt for me was written all over his face. He added insult to injury by not only giving me that look but shaking his head at the same time. I had never been so easily reduced to a feeling of defeat than I was by this action. After all, he was a human being and he was treating me with utter worthlessness. It was almost a physical blow.

He seemed to reserve this look and action for me. It became a real challenge to ignore it and move on. Just when I was asking "How much more can I take?" there was more. This look became a regular occurrence in my home, in my car, in my yard.

Contempt in the Classroom

It wouldn't be long, however, until Ian's looks weren't exclusively reserved for me. The teachers began seeing these looks in the classroom. It became part of his reaction to corrective criticism and it totally surprised them. Until this point, he had been a pleasant, cooperative student. Now he was becoming more arrogant and aloof. It was a sign of things to come at school. All part of the journey.

Again I found myself looking to the future. I imagined him older, bigger, stronger, and treating his family, teachers, and authority figures with such utter disrespect. The prospect was quite depressing. I knew that if we didn't find the right treatment, the future was bleak.

The Little Bully

It was right about this time that I truly questioned whether I could continue to live in the fight or flight mode. Ian was now eight years old and problems were beginning to show up at school.

His physical education teachers sent a note home, explaining that he was very disrespectful during class, refusing to do what they had asked of him. This, from a very athletic boy who loved sports! We were asked to schedule a conference with his homeroom teachers and the physical education teachers. They went on to say that he had given them glaring, defiant looks. He was now in the habit of muttering under his breath how "stupid" everyone was. They got that too.

In the weeks to come, two bus conduct reports were sent home as well. Ian was now becoming known as a bully. Well, that's basically what he had been at home: a bully. He was aggressive, frustrated, angry, and violent. Our family avoided confrontations with him. He was really running the show. I thought, *When will this stop?* It stopped one day when we came to the end of the road.

As I was driving Ian home from an after-school activity, he was having a tantrum in the passenger seat of my car. (This, mind you, was only a one-mile trip.) What was it about? Was he overtired? Hungry? Angry at someone? Angry about something that happened? I didn't know and it didn't really matter. There was no talking to him now. He was spinning out of control and words did not help the matter one bit. He was screaming at me with disgust, kicking the seats, hitting the car window, and kicking the dashboard.

I was afraid he would lunge at me as I drove. Then something clicked. I'd had it. I turned off the road onto a residential side street. I put the car in park, hit the unlock button, and ran around the back of the car to his passenger door. He must have anticipated what was coming because he tried to climb over the center console and get out my driver's side door. I was quicker this time. I pulled him out of the car and jumped into his seat. I shut the door and hit the door locks. I threw myself back behind the steering wheel, I slammed my door, and I drove away. Yes, I left my son on the side of a road. And it felt great. I drove down a few blocks, turned down a couple of streets, and never looked back. I pulled over, shaking, and prayed. I was there several minutes. I drove a different route home.

I pulled into my garage, shut the door, and went inside. I calmly said hello to Roger and Abby and sat down at the kitchen counter. I asked them if Ian was home, prompting some confusion, as I had just left to pick him up. Right about that time, Ian came in. He was in a much better place. I later discovered that he had walked home through the desert following the road we had been driving on. The walk gave him much- needed time to calm down and provided an adventure as well. He didn't say anything to me and calmly went into his room. I briefly explained to my family what had taken place. They looked at me with baffled expressions. I guess you just had to be there.

Terrorism

My family had been living in turmoil for years and it was showing on all of us. I continued to struggle with isolation and depression. I believe my husband, a very positive individual, was overwhelmed and bordering on depression himself. My daughter was making herself scarce and clearly struggling to sort it all out. And my son was miserable. My search for respite care had not come up with any results yet.

Looking back, I remembered that one of the therapists had compared our home life to living with terrorism. Just as our country and world now feared terrorism after September 11, 2001, I feared an attack at any moment in my own home. I was physically afraid of my son and ashamed to admit it. How could I be afraid of an eight-year-old boy? Let me tell you.

The Ambush

One typical afternoon, my children came home from school and Ian was visibly upset about something. Abby and I were in the kitchen, and Ian came out in a rage and making demands. I didn't understand what had set him off. I knew he needed to calm himself down and quickly. I sent him to his room to cool off. He refused and started to become aggressive. He wanted to engage me in a physical fight. I took him by the arm and physically dragged him down the hallway to his room. With him on the floor in his room, I shut the door and walked back to the kitchen.

As I was walking through the kitchen, Abby said, "Mom, watch out! He's right behind you!" I turned around in time to see Ian, pure contempt and rage on his face, lunging at me with both fists clenched. I dragged him again to his room and shut the door. He would not leave the door closed and kept running after me. By this point, Abby was clearly shaken over what she had just witnessed. I could not control my son. I wasn't strong enough physically or emotionally. Afraid of an eight-year-old boy? You bet.

14
Searching for Answers

After the behavioral spikes, life for Ian settled down somewhat. He continued to have trouble sleeping and, as a result, was edgy. When watching a television program, he could not sit still, he was always moving. When writing, he would grip the pencil very tightly, and each letter had to be perfect. If it wasn't, he would become angry, rip up the paper, and break the pencil in half. He was easily agitated and angry. The anti-depressant didn't seem as effective as it had once been.

We went back to the pediatrician and discussed alternative medications. Willing to try another medication, we began with a low dose of the stimulant medication used for children with ADD and ADHD as part of an overall treatment regimen. I knew of some children who were taking it with great success. One of the positive benefits of this medication was its timed-release action, eliminating trips to the nurse's office for medication during school.

Even with the Best of Intentions

I've learned so many lessons along the way. I've learned that for parents, caregivers, and physicians this world of pediatric medication is a learn-as-you-go process. What works for one child may not work for another. As Dr. Trunzo stated, "Parents need to approach treatment knowing that there are no magic pills. You try all of it, from psychologists to pediatricians, from nutritionists to medications. With medication, you may hit it lucky with the first attempt, or you may need to try all twenty different medications. The bottom line is you don't give up trying."

In our case we discovered that the stimulant medication had a negative impact on Ian. He became even more agitated, nervous, and mean. I didn't like what we were seeing with this treatment. After talking with Dr. Trunzo, we stopped this new medication and increased the original medication slightly. We had had success with this in the past and decided to stick with it for now.

Individuals are biologically different from one another; therefore, medications will affect people differently. On several occasions, I've heard parents complain that they tried a medication and it didn't help. Some have even commented that a certain medication made things worse, and they adamantly refuse to ever try another. This situation is exactly what Dr. Trunzo was referring to. We simply cannot give up. The right diagnosis coupled with the right treatment can give a child the opportunity to gain self-control and calm down. In some cases, it makes a night-and-day difference. While I certainly disagree with the doctors who are quick to write a prescription, I also disagree with the concept of never considering medications to help kids. There are medications out there that are possibly the exact thing your child needs. I was about to learn that. Not yet, though.

Ian was now eight years old and I was questioning what the outlook for his future was. I had been saying since he was a toddler that I needed help, that something was wrong. I also had been saying for years that I want to help him before he is five, before he is eight, before he is ten and violent. The years were passing, he was growing, and I didn't feel we had helped him enough yet. There had to be more.

Searching the Web

I began searching the Internet for anything that could lead to answers on how to effectively parent and help Ian. I would spend hours at time gathering information, printing articles, highlighting important details. I compiled a file of ODD research and learned about a variety of disorders from learning disabilities to bipolar disorder. In my research the latter, bipolar disorder, took me in a new direction.

The National Institute of Mental Health gives a cautionary note on antidepressants and stimulants on the website for the Child and Adolescent Bipolar Foundation at www.bpkids.org: "Using stimulant medications to treat attention deficit hyperactivity disorder (ADHD) or ADHD-like symptoms in a child with bipolar disorder may worsen manic symptoms." My first thought was, "Does my son really have bipolar disorder, and the medications have been making his symptoms worse?"

In further reading, I discovered that many characteristics matched Ian's current behaviors. While I agreed that he needed medication to treat his disorder, I began questioning whether we had the proper diagnosis and were using the right medications. And what if we were dealing with something more? The questions and concerns were mounting. How many parents were going through something like this? I was about to learn how many disorders have similar characteristics and symptoms.

During this time my sister Kathy and I were in daily contact via phone calls and emails. I was discussing my findings on bipolar disorder and medications when I learned that Kathy had been questioning the very same thing. In her reading and conversations 2,000 miles away, she had come across the same theory. I believe sisters have a real connection to each other. This proved it.

We Need Support

In my continued search for understanding of ODD, I discovered Dr. Ross Green's book, *The Explosive Child*. This was the first book I found that dealt specifically with defiance. After reading it cover to cover, I went to the website www.explosivekids.org and discovered a lifeline to other individuals struggling with consequences of ODD.

This site took me to Parents and Teachers of Explosive Kids (PTEK), a parent and teacher support group for working with behaviorally challenging children. I spent hours on this site, reading articles and other parents' stories of life with defiant children. It was both enlightening and heartbreaking at the same time: enlightening to know we weren't alone, heartbreaking because I could hear the desperation in their words. Several of the stories were almost mirror images of what we were facing. I can still picture myself sitting in front of a glowing computer screen late at night while my family slept, tears silently falling as I read the words of so many desperate, struggling people looking for answers to help their children.

Home Is Where the Hostility Is

I found another affirming article at www.conductdisorders.com, which addressed ODD. It stated that "ODD is persistent disobedience and opposition to authority figures." I think we all agree on that. It went on to say that "The basic rights of individuals were still respected and age-appropriate societal rules and behaviors were not violated." Hence, the good behavior and generally good relationship interaction with peers.

Here's where it hits home, if you'll pardon the pun! As Dr. Douglas A. Riley stated in his book, *The Defiant Child*, "ODD is characterized by negative, hostile, and defiant behaviors, generally strongest in the home." Thank you! Finally someone describes this baffling thing called oppositional defiant disorder.

This behavior will eventually spill over into the school setting. Even more serious, if not treated properly, the behavior has the potential to develop into something worse: conduct disorder.

Conduct Disorder:
Oppositional Defiant Disorder All Grown Up

Conduct disorder is defined by the *DSM-IV-TR*, as a repetitive and persistent pattern of behavior in which the basic rights of others or major age-appropriate societal norms or rules are violated, as manifested by the presence of three (or more) of the following criteria in the past 12 months, with at least one criterion present in the past 6 months:

- *Aggression to people and animals*
- *Destruction of property*
- *Deceitfulness or theft*
- *Serious violations of rules (p. 98-99)*

The *DSM-IV-TR* states "In a significant proportion of cases, Oppositional Defiant Disorder is a developmental antecedent to Conduct Disorder. Children with oppositional defiant disorder typically do not include aggression toward people or animals, destruction of property, or a pattern of theft or deceit" (p. 101-102)*.

In the past, these children were referred to as "juvenile delinquents." Where the child with ODD may tease a dog, the child with CD will actually torture it. The child with ODD may say he hates the police; the child with CD will spray paint obscene graffiti on the police station. A child with ODD will refuse to go to bed; the child with CD will stay out all night. You get the idea.

The link between the two disorders is the issue of safety. Kids with CD present serious safety concerns for themselves, their families, their classmates, their teachers, and their community. They also present safety issues for the property of those individuals. CD, like ODD, rarely exists alone. After a child has been examined, another disorder is oftentimes discovered to be present, referred to as comorbid or coexisting conditions.

After all those years of telling doctors I didn't want my son to continue on this destructive path, I now had a name for what I wanted to prevent: conduct disorder. The child with CD is in need of immediate help. While the scope of this book does not include CD, it needs to be mentioned so that parents and caregivers are aware of potential future problems.

*Reprinted with permission from the Diagnostic and Statistical Manual of Mental Disorders, Copyright 2000. American Psychiatric Association.

15

Words of Affirmation

As the winter holidays approached, I began to feel displaced. Not having established a network of friends in our new city yet, the holiday invitations weren't exactly rolling in. In previous years our social calendar for the month of December included everything from making gingerbread houses at the community center to fancy catered events with a hundred guests. The loneliness I was experiencing, coupled with the incredible tension in our household, was almost too much to bear. My sister sensed this isolation 2,000 miles away and called. "Nan, I think you need to come home this Christmas. You need to be with your family. Let's get you all back for a week to share in the Christmas season." This was the beginning of my sister's stepping into action on my behalf.

I have a framed picture of Kathy and me, taken at her son's wedding. The inscription on the frame reads "Sisters...they are blessed with an extra sense that whispers when the other needs them," A. Danielson. My sisters and I are blessed with that extra sense and I am so thankful.

Planning a winter vacation when you live in a warm climate year round presents some challenges. My children had long since grown out of their winter coats, hats, boots, and sweaters. How would I outfit them for a one-week period? Already one step ahead of me, Kathy sent out an email to her network of friends asking for extra winter clothes in our kids' sizes. Within a week of planning the trip, we had complete winter outfits for our entire family, from hats to boots!

After being "Home for the Holidays" to visit family, Kathy invited me to stay on with her at her home, Hybanks, for her birthday celebration. She had invited my other sisters and her close women friends for a weekend retreat. With my husband's blessing, I sent my family to the airport (in a blizzard; they considered it an adventure), while I stayed on for the weekend bonus. Here I was, in the depths of despair, about to spend a weekend with sisters and women friends. It had been so long since I really felt joy. I wasn't sure I could find it again. Worse yet, I had been isolated for so long, I wasn't sure if I knew how to "be" around this group of people: how to act. I quickly realized that these women were a precious gift to me. They were open and caring, and they truly made me feel welcome. I was sharing fellowship and being comforted. It was totally spontaneous, not at all planned. It was just what I needed.

During this time I had the privilege of meeting Dr. Susan Youngs, medical director of the Program for Exceptional Families at Oakwood Healthcare System in Michigan. Dr. Youngs' heart for special children and their families was obvious to everyone around her. She was not only a pediatrician, she was a close friend of my sister Kathy. I believe it was a divine appointment that brought us together that cold winter weekend in Spring Lake.

As the Michigan winter swirled outside, Susan and I shared conversation and insights. We sat on a cozy window seat covered with floral print pillows in front of the huge window overlooking the lake. The fireplace was going, and women were sharing laughter and conversation all about the house. It was such a precious time for me. I discovered that Susan worked with special-needs kids in her practice. She shared her story of becoming a doctor and having a missionary heart, which took her to Vellore, India; Gabon, Africa; and the Dominican Republic. Yes, she did indeed have a missionary heart.

As we spoke, I began to feel that she understood the anguish I was living with. Susan spoke these life-changing words to me: "I work with autism and physically challenged kids and their parents. I see what they live and experience on a day-to-day basis. I can say that what you are living, with ODD and its effects, is the hardest to deal with. It's hard because other people simply do not, cannot, understand it unless they've lived it." Wow! No one had ever, ever said anything like that to me during my years of searching for help. Of course, that doesn't minimize the struggles parents experience raising kids with serious physical disabilities. It simply affirmed the fact that ODD and other behavioral disorders are also serious disabilities— they're just not quite as obvious. And they're often misunderstood when the outward signs are there; parents are often judged to be inept in raising their child. What adds to the frustration is that there are fewer resources and less information on ODD compared to the information and support available for families coping with physical disabilities. In a very real way, her comments validated me as a mother dealing with the family dynamics of living with ODD and its effects.

This was the beginning of my friendship with Dr. Youngs. Throughout the next two years, we communicated via email regarding Ian's progress. I could turn to her in the middle of the night and write a desperate email inquiring about medications, doctors, and parenting. As busy as she was with her own family, her practice, and her community service, she always took time to write back. That communication was a lifeline to me.

Dr. Youngs was excited and supportive when I informed her that I was writing this book. She pointed out the need for a book written by a parent for parents in raising special kids. In fact, not long after that, she asked for my insights regarding a nine-year-old patient of hers. This young girl was exhibiting signs of ODD and possibly conduct disorder. Could I summarize what my doctor had done for my son? Could I also recommend organizations and websites that would be helpful for this family? I was honored that she would be asking for my input. Once again, Dr. Youngs gave encouragement. This time, she affirmed me in writing this book for parents.

16

It Takes a Village

As is common in kids with ODD, the teachers at school had had no concerns regarding Ian's behavior and school performance. That changed at the end of first grade and the start of second grade. Up until then, he was fine at school, on sports teams, and in school activities. It was at home that he became totally defiant, compulsive, and uncontrollable. This is a pattern that often-times adds to a parent's feeling of inadequacy. If he is so good at school and in those other situations, what is it about our family that makes him act this way? Take heart, however, that most parents of kids with ODD feel this way. Also, the behavior will eventually spill over into schoolwork. It's just a matter of time.

At this point, I still had not confided in Ian's teachers that he had ODD. I did not indicate the medications he was on when filling out his emergency medical card, filed in the nurse's office. I had worked in the schools. I knew that "Confidential" didn't always mean confidential. I was fearful of volunteers seeing his medical records. I didn't want him labeled by parents, administrators, teachers, and students. I was still protecting him at all costs. I justified it by telling myself he does not take any meds while he is in school. My home, work, and cell phone numbers were all on the card. If an emergency arose, I could be reached. I chose not to disclose the information.

It was all unraveling, though. Our home life was somewhat improved with the medication. But Ian was eight years old now, bigger, and stronger. He still was not happy and well-adjusted. He continued to withhold affection. I hadn't heard an "I love you" in years. Yes, years. We were all weary and it was showing. When his teacher called for a conference, Roger and I agreed it was time to discuss Ian's medical history, ask for advice, and receive a promise from the teachers to keep the conversation between us. I even went so far as to request that they not take any notes. I felt both relieved and scared. It was a leap of faith, a turning point for us all.

Teachers Really Do Make a Difference

On a late afternoon, we met with Ian's teachers, Susan Dankberg and Paula Charnicki. They were both concerned and wanted to help. We entered the room with anxiety; we left the room with new hope.

While I had always respected his teachers, I hadn't realized the great resource and support I especially had in Ian's teacher, Susan Dankberg. Mrs. Dankberg had twenty-four years of teaching experience in addition to having raised her own two sons. Also, being a member of her school's Student Study Team during the past eight years had given her a variety of experiences with teachers and parents working to resolve students' academic and behavioral concerns.

This dynamic teacher, with her New York accent and professional style, gave my family the direction we had so desperately sought. During a one-hour conference, we discussed eight years' worth of struggles to help Ian. I was prepared and summarized rather quickly, giving the main points of the journey we had been on. Surprisingly, I was not emotional; rather, I felt detached, as if I were telling someone else's story. It did, however, feel like a release of sorts. I was beginning to let people in. I was asking for help and direction from the teachers. And most important, they were listening. In fact, Susan Dankberg would become a trusted friend and mentor during the following years.

The teachers agreed to simply discuss Ian's behavior and not make a written record of his medical history. That would remain between the parents and the teachers. I will always be grateful for their keeping our confidence. I'll always be grateful, too, for their honesty. After three years of glowing teacher reports on what a pleasure my son was to have in class, I was actually glad to hear he had been acting out. He had been giving teachers the look of contempt I had been receiving. He was arrogant and refusing to do his work. This stunned the teachers. Was there something going on at home? Problems? Medical condition? I was relieved that someone else besides our family was seeing this.

In addition to the teacher conference, I had scheduled an appointment with a well-known pediatric neurologist on staff at a local hospital. We planned to talk with the teachers and also to try a new doctor. I had searched the Internet for local pediatric physicians who work with behavioral and chemical imbalances. I was ready to see yet another doctor.

Fortunately, in talking with the teachers, who were compassionate and empathetic, I discussed this upcoming appointment. We saw the hesitation in Mrs. Dankberg's eyes. She didn't want to tell us what to do, but she had seen the results of this doctor's work with students in the past. He tended to overmedicate and she did not like his treatment plan. I respected her opinion and was totally open to, and thankful for, her advice. We decided right then and there to cancel that appointment.

This teacher meeting was so important to us. I saw the look of compassion on both Mrs. Charnicki's and Mrs. Dankberg's faces. Furthermore, Mrs. Dankberg had experience with defiant children, had empathy for us (especially for me as the mom), and most important, had a referral. She gave us the name of a doctor who specialized in neurology and clinical neurophysiology. She described him as taking a conservative approach to medications. He had helped children she knew personally, was a professor at the local university, and was a respected leader in his field. I made the appointment when we returned home. That was the single most important phone call I've ever made.

The teachers were thankful that we had opened up about our son, their student. I realized too, that, by my explaining our struggles to his teachers, Ian had more support and understanding from them as well. Rather than thinking he just had an attitude, they knew he was struggling with a serious problem. Why had I waited so long? It was all part of the journey.

In addition to the valuable resources of teachers, I have discovered that many schools offer prevention and counseling services to their students and families. In my city, for example, Scottsdale Prevention Institute (SPI), a non-profit organization, offers prevention, intervention, and support for individuals ages five to eighteen. SPI works to promote well-being by offering a wide variety of services, including parenting workshops, programs on divorce adjustment, coping skills, anger management, and chemical awareness. SPI's mission statement is, "To advocate and provide substance abuse and mental health prevention services that will improve the quality of life and well-being of children and families." They continue to state their belief that "the entire community is needed to keep our children drug free and healthy."

In order to be successful advocates for our children, we need to seek out services like SPI. A good place to start is within our own public schools. School nurses, psychologists, teachers, and office staff should be familiar with services offered. Many prevention programs are offered at no cost, or minimal cost, and are funded by private foundations and individual donations. These organizations provided valuable resources to parents raising children in today's world. Whether we are raising a challenging child or facing a crisis within our family, prevention and counseling services can provide us with techniques and strategies to help us through.

17

Rescue Angels

It was around this time in the journey that I learned what the term "respite care" really means to a family. Respite care refers to temporary child care that is provided by people who are familiar with the specific needs of your child. This care can range from as little as one hour to several months, depending on the family's situation. There are also respite care centers, organizations, and state and federal agencies that offer this service. Your physician is a good starting place for respite referrals. The cost for respite care may be covered in several ways, including public assistance, private insurance, volunteer organizations, and private pay.

It sounds wonderful, but as with all child care, finding quality respite care for your child is not easy, and oftentimes can be quite overwhelming. I learned this firsthand when, exhausted and desperate, I began my search. I then discovered that respite can come in the form of the gift of time from a neighbor, a friend, a relative, or a babysitter. *Merriam-Webster's Collegiate Dictionary* defines respite as "a period of temporary delay, a reprieve; an interval of rest or relief." A reprieve! Rest and relief! Boy, did we all need that! Living out-of-state from our immediate family and closest friends, I never felt we had an option of respite care. In a time when so many families are mobile, we often find ourselves feeling even more isolated when caring for a special child.

About the time I began letting people in, my sister and mentor who had been my only confidante outside of my immediate family, literally became one of my "Rescue Angels." She not only encouraged me to seek help, she lifted me in prayer and gave me the love and support I so desperately needed. Just when I was ready to collapse from surviving yet another tantrum, from being screamed at, from pure exhaustion, I would open my mail to find a card from Kathy. After I had discovered Max Lucado's *In the Eye of the Storm* at Hybanks, Kathy proceeded to slowly but steadily build my collection of Max Lucado books; he is her favorite author and is now mine too. One envelope contained a little book by Stormie Omartian, *Just Enough Light for the Step I'm On.* If that one sounds inspirational, that's because it was!

Along the way, during the past year when life had become truly dysfunctional in our family, I opened up to how difficult the situation was. I confided to her that I have said to each and every doctor and therapist, "I can't do this anymore," only to be sent home with little hope for better days. My sister truly listened with an open heart. She did not judge, claim to understand, or offer advice. Instead she listened, loved, and cared. Through the power of prayer and a plan of action, she rescued me.

She began by calling and talking with my daughter. She got the dates for our upcoming spring break and made plans to fly Ian home to family for a week of respite care. Kathy discussed the plan with my sister Judy, and they both became my "Rescue Angels," devising a plan of activities and care for Ian for one full week! He would get to spend time with his grandparents, aunts, uncles, cousins and friends. What a gift!

As parents of children with ODD, we realize babysitters are not usually an option. We all have horror stories to share of out-of-control children in the care of an overwhelmed, baffled, and often tearful babysitter. In our case, we once even had the father of the babysitter come over. To add a little humor to this story, the father also happened to be a police officer for our city! Ugly stuff to deal with, and seeing these neighbors every day adds more embarrassment to the situation. And the isolation continues to grow.

Babysitters were non-existent for us and respite care was elusive. With preliminary searching, I found programs do exist. At the point where I was researching online for respite care, my sisters stepped in and gave us the respite, reprieve, and relief that we desperately needed. It was truly a lifeline to us.

Not only was it healthy for us as parents, and for our teenage daughter, it was healthy for our son. He needed the break from us as well. It was such a gift to our family. If immediate family or friends are not an option for respite care, it is important to explore outside sources. Respite is available for small intervals of time or longer periods. I've included a Resource Guide at the back of the book, which includes sources of respite care.

18

Hostile Mom in the Waiting Room

After years of pediatricians, family physicians, and therapists we found ourselves in yet another doctor's office. The appointment was scheduled for a weekday, so we pulled Ian out of school. Mrs. Dankberg understood why and was glad to know we had followed through with her recommendation. I was told it would be a full day, meaning three hours in the morning, a break for lunch, then three hours in the afternoon. We had spent a day like this before, at the pediatric neuropsychologist's office in early 2002. I knew we were in for a long day. I prayed that Ian would have enough stamina and would cooperate. He had always done his best in these situations, and he once again showed his fiercely competitive personality. He wanted to be the best.

Again, I was faced with the task of "filling out some forms" before the consultation. I was at once excited and hopeful, yet hostile and frustrated. I was excited and hopeful to be meeting the doctor so highly recommended by Ian's teacher. I was frustrated because I'd filled out what seemed like hundreds of these parent surveys. And finally, I was feeling hostile as I let the fear in the pit of my stomach take over. Could this doctor help my son?

If I Had Only Known

When the office staff gave me the familiar clipboard, pen, and papers, I was less than pleasant. I was becoming agitated. I complained to my husband that we hadn't even met the doctor yet, and I was spending time answering a hundred questions.

As I glanced at my defiant son sitting across from me, I reached my limit. I said, "I'm not doing this. Not until we've at least met this doctor." I marched up to the receptionist and proceeded to tell her, "I can't do this. I'm exhausted and I just want my son to see the doctor. This is overwhelming to me. We've been to countless doctors and I've filled out these things so many times. I just can't do this. I'm sorry." I handed her the clipboard.

Looking a little bewildered, she kindly said that she would talk to the doctor. After giving me some time, she came back and explained gently that it was very important to complete the forms. The doctor needed the background information to use in the consultation. She assured me I had plenty of time and asked me if I would like some tea.

If I had only taken the time to read over the materials presented to us, I would have understood the importance of those questions. They weren't basic health history questions. I was completing a Parent Rating Scale, the Achenbach Child Behavior Checklist, and a Children's Depression Index. This data would become a vital part of what is referred to as a qualitative academic and a quantitative neurological examination.

I completed all the questions. Then I had some tea.

We Begin—Again

We were ready to meet Dr. Drake D. Duane, Director of the Institute for Developmental Behavioral Neurology. Dr. Duane's educational background, achievements, and positions held were very impressive. Could he help Ian? We were about to learn that, yes, indeed, this doctor could help all of us. We discovered the long-awaited direction, guidance, and treatment we had been desperately searching for.

Ian wasn't looking forward to the day of testing but had a surprisingly good attitude. Again, he started the day with a competitive outlook. Tests? You bet. Bring 'em on! He was ready for computer games that tested his skills and puzzles that challenged his mind. He'd been through this before. He could do it again. This day, however, would be much different. We were about to find out just how different.

After the office staff settled down that hostile mom in the waiting room (oh yes, that was me), Ian was called into the doctor's office to meet Dr. Duane. Following the consultation, he would be undergoing various diagnostic studies.

In the meantime Roger and I were asked into a small, comfortable room to view an educational videotape exploring various developmental and neurological disorders. We were also given reprints of several publications written by Dr. Duane and other experts in the field of behavioral neurology. We were in a room filled with books and materials on everything from dyslexia to Parkinson's disease. I didn't know where to begin! I wanted to view the tape, read the articles, and read the books all at once! (Thankfully, Dr. Duane allowed us to borrow the videotape). Anything I could find on oppositional defiant disorder? Yes. I found myself in a library filled with incredible resources. I wanted to gain as much insight as possible. I was beginning to feel confident that we were in the right place. Finally.

We were called to join in the consultation. Upon meeting Dr. Duane, it was apparent that he was a man who was esteemed in his field and who had the gift of putting people at ease. He was a commanding man, well-spoken and intelligent. He started off by smiling and saying how much he enjoyed talking with Ian. He clearly liked Ian and wanted to help him. I felt assured in his presence that things were going to get better.

During the meeting, the doctor reviewed Ian's developmental history. He asked questions regarding my pregnancy, the delivery, and the first few days of Ian's life. How was he? Did he cry often? Was he a happy baby? What were his sleep patterns? How was his appetite? As we talked, it became apparent that things weren't easy from the very start with our son. We knew that. Now we were verbalizing that fact with a doctor who understood. He posed a key question to us: "What does that tell you about your son?" Silence. Tired expressions.

He waited for a reply. He then stated, "Your son, from the start, was biologically different." He didn't respond to stimuli like our daughter had. He didn't react to holding and soothing like our daughter had. He was biologically different from the first child we had; our parenting methods had different results with him. The doctor stated that our son was biologically different, possibly because of a chemical imbalance in the brain. By testing him in three distinct areas, we could gather data that would, we hoped, lead us to an accurate diagnosis and effective treatment. These tests included: physiological studies (addressing physical functioning), cognitive assessments (related to thinking or knowing), and psychological studies (related to mental functioning).

Through physiological studies, we would discern how Ian's brain functioned physiologically, or electrically, through tests such as an electroencephalogram. This would involve a computer-assisted assessment during which Ian would get to relax and at one point even fall asleep. Blood work, including testing for blood sugars, cholesterol, muscle enzymes, thyroid, and lead levels was done. Unfortunately, he didn't sleep through that test; however, he was very cooperative!

Through cognitive assessments, that include measures of attention, memory, and perceptual motor function, we would determine how Ian deals with visual and auditory information. This would be fun for Ian. He would use several games, including interactive computer programs, puzzles, and word challenges.

Finally, through psychological studies, we could assess Ian's mood, anxiety, and personality traits that may impact a variety of developmental and neurological problems. This is where all that parent information comes in. The Parent Rating Scales, the Achenbach Child Behavior Checklist, and the Children's Depression Index all give essential information to the neurologist as he assesses Ian's psychological state.

Were we ready? Yes. Was Ian ready? Yes. For my son, the testing began—again. For us, the wait began—again. How many hours have we spent waiting? Countless. Somehow, this time was going to be different. It just had to be.

"Mom, does this mean...?"

What followed that day was a morning of testing, a break for lunch, and an afternoon of testing. Here was a boy who could be defiant beyond imagination, yet he was cooperating with these individuals he had never met before. As the hours passed, I prayed that he would last through the day. I was amazed by the way he handled it all. How was Ian managing to control his impulsiveness and anger during these tests? He was being questioned, challenged, and poked with a needle. He didn't really want to be here. How was he doing it? When he took a break for lunch, I had my answer.

At the end of the morning session, he entered the waiting room, and we prepared to leave for lunch. He looked tired, but surprisingly not frustrated. As he took my hand, he looked up at me. I leaned down to hear him quietly ask the question that will stay with me forever, "Mom, does this mean I won't be mean anymore?"

A Strong Finish

After the last test was completed, Roger and I met with the doctor. He smiled as he relayed highlights from his conversations with our son. He found Ian to be bright, intense, and serious. They shared stories of sports and school. All testing had gone well and we could expect to have the results the following week. In the meantime, we discussed the recent years leading us to this point.

Giving the doctor examples of Ian's extreme behaviors, we cited several recent episodes. The common one: We're at a stop light, and he leans in from the back seat to say, "Dad, the light is red. When it turns green, go! Let's make it home by 4:45!" To which my husband would reply, "Son, it is 4:41, the light is red, and we won't make it to our house by then." The following minutes would be filled with tension and building rage as Ian, regardless of our comments, insists on pulling into our driveway before the clock hits 4:45. By the time we do arrive, he is in a full-blown rage, either kicking and hitting the seats or refusing to get out of the car and come into the house.

Interestingly, as we told this story, Dr. Duane smiled and shook his head in agreement. He knew our son! After several more stories, we realized that this doctor did indeed know Ian and his condition. What excitement for us! Someone who really had a handle on this erratic behavior! Someone who was knowledgeable and gave us hope.

The day ended later than expected. We didn't actually leave the neurologist's office until six o'clock. It's safe to say all three of us were exhausted. But we left there with something we didn't have that same morning: an understanding doctor and the promise of better days.

Ian could take his trip to visit family and we could have our week of respite. During that time, Dr. Duane would gather and interpret all the assessment and evaluation data on our son. We scheduled a wrap-up session when we would review the results. We would also receive a copy of the doctor's dictated report for our records. It was the beginning of successful treatment for a young boy who no longer wanted to "be mean." We were on our way.

19

A New Perspective

We waited at the airport until the flight monitor indicated that Ian's flight was listed as "en route." Like our son, we were en route: on our way to a week of respite! The only word to describe what I was feeling at that moment is "relief." It was freeing to know that someone else, someone whom I loved and trusted, would be caring for Ian.

I had never really thought of what we would do when Ian was away and we were given a period of respite. Oftentimes when the days were bad, I would escape to my room and sleep. This was an indicator of my depression, along with the reality of pure physical exhaustion. Did I want to sleep the entire week my son was away? No. Did I want to take my husband's suggestion and fly to Las Vegas for a few days? No. There had to be a healthy balance between the two options. The challenge was to find it, and fast. We only had one week.

On our first evening, we went out to dinner. We enjoyed some wine and a very nice meal. But the entire time I was there, I felt like I was watching the scene from a distance. All I really wanted to do was "be." I needed to just have quiet time. Peace. Time to reflect and relax. My husband had suggested a variety of ways to spend our week: dinners out, movies, and trips. I didn't want to hurt his feelings; this was his week too. I compared this to a reentry into society. We had been away for a long time; I didn't really know where to begin.

Wanting to spend time with Abby, now fifteen, we invited her to dinner. We joked with her that now we could give her our undivided attention for the whole week. I think we made her a little nervous!

We both looked across the table at our beautiful young daughter and realized how much time we had missed with her. Yet, she was there, healthy and laughing with us. She was embarrassed, however, to be out with her parents on a Friday night! I thought, so many missed moments with our girl, so many missed moments as a family. Then I was given this verse from the Bible, "I will repay you for the years the locusts have eaten" (Joel 2:25). I believe that, through this journey, God has promised that there is still hope. My lost years can be used for good. What I've learned from the past ten years can help others. That purpose has become so clear to me.

What I learned regarding Abby from our respite week was that her life hadn't slowed down as we struggled with Ian. She had grown up right in front of my eyes. Only, my eyes had been so very tired through the years. Holidays, birthdays, special occasions, and everyday events were unique challenges to our family. Some were definitely better than others. Some were fun. Others were very disappointing. Through it all, I tried to keep the traditions up and keep the joy in the moment rather than in the entire day. That helped. Moments can be magical. Moments can be attainable. Sometimes, the moment is all we have.

Self-Reliance

With time, I was also able to see Abby and reflect on how she has grown. I was concerned about the dysfunctional years she had lived through. How would they shape the woman she would become? The wife she would become? The mom she would become? There were countless disappointments and heartbreaks over the years. There was daily chaos in the household. She had seen and heard things that I'm afraid she'll never forget.

I had taken my concerns to the behavioral therapist. He assured me that Abby would be stronger in many ways. She would be more independent, flexible, and sensitive to the needs of others, he said. I hoped so.

In my heart, I knew she was watching how I responded to things.

I kept telling myself to model the best possible behavior I could drum up at the time, under the circumstances. I needed to teach her that a mother's love knows no boundaries. That mothers don't stop trying. She was watching me. She was learning from me. How would I handle it? With grace and patience? With faith? Or would I fail miserably in her eyes?

In the meantime, my prayer for her has always been that she would know that families do not give up on each other. No matter what. I also pray that in her eyes, when she reflects on her childhood, she would see a mom who loved her and her brother, who was dedicated to her family, and who trusted God to see us all through. No matter what.

Blessed Are the Peacemakers

I've come to view Abby as the peacemaker in our family. In retrospect, it was she who tried to smooth things over as they were falling apart. From the time we told her our news about her new baby brother, all she wanted was to love him. His disorder made that very challenging, especially for a young girl. Yet, she didn't give up on him.

Yes, there were very dark moments in which she admitted her deepest resentments over Ian's actions. Those moments were few. Actually, too few. More often than not, she would try to change the subject or offer praise or words of encouragement. She would give me distance when she saw my frustration building. In fact, she gave me too much distance. She retreated into her room, where she felt safe.

Then again, there were times when she would chime in, particularly after one of my son's tantrums, and tell of a project on which she had received an "A" or of an award she got in art class. Her accomplishments were dimmed by the atmosphere in which they were shared. I didn't have much left to give. At one point, I remember telling her, as kindly as I could, that it was best if she wait to talk with me for just a few minutes after a tantrum had occurred. She said she understood. I wonder if she did.

Each Day our Own

During our week of respite we were able to take each day and use it to renew, rest, and recharge. And that's exactly what we did. We enjoyed dinner out every night (much to my husband's delight) and spent time with our daughter. It still seemed surreal, this new life for a week, but I was beginning to settle in. I spent time reading my devotionals, enjoying coffee, and writing. I took the time to enjoy the beautiful surroundings my husband had worked so hard on—the Southwestern gardens, the patio, and the courtyard. All were peaceful places to reflect and enjoy the solitude.

We caught up on projects around the house. We even made that long-talked-about appointment with an attorney to draw up new wills. So many things we did not have time or energy for before! With a challenging child, the main goal of each day is simply doing your best to get through it. The agenda changes. Details fall by the wayside. For two such detail-oriented people as my husband and me, this was very frustrating. So, part of the gift of the respite week was being able to get things in order and pay attention to some long-neglected details.

A Father's Fears

It was during our meeting with our attorney that I gained new insight into my husband's struggle and new insights into his heart. We were discussing what every parent fears—what would happen to our children if we both died? Keeping in mind that we had been on this eight-year journey and still hadn't found the right treatment for Ian, the prospect of not being here for him was frightening. Who could care for him and possibly begin to understand what he's all about? We were blessed with a family who would be there to take guardianship but how would they manage it all? We loved him, we were devoted to him, and we still didn't have things under control. Our fears weren't so much for the immediate future as for the long-term outlook for him. What would his future hold? Would he and his sister be there for each other?

"Train a child in the way he should go, and when he is old, he will not turn from it" (Proverbs 22:6). Looking at Roger's face, I saw it all clearly. His heart's desire was to raise this young boy into a man of character. But years of fear and doubt had taken their toll. We are thankful that with the advice and compassion from good counsel, we were able to successfully plan for our children's future in the event we were deceased. And soon, this father's fears would be replaced by hope and plans for a brighter future for Ian and our family.

20

The Road Less Traveled

omething big was happening in our country around this time. In churches across America, pastors were giving weekly sermons on living "the purpose driven life."

A book of the same title, *The Purpose Driven Life: What on Earth am I Here For?* by Rick Warren, had been #1 on the New York Times bestseller list since its publication in 2002.

Copies of the book and the accompanying study guide were everywhere! This wasn't appealing to Christian groups exclusively. It was appealing to a cross-section of America. It seemed everybody had heard of this book. In a phone call, my sister Judy commented that her college-age daughter had just finished reading it and could not put it down. I thought, "There must be something to this," and as they say "timing is everything."

Pastors encouraged individuals to read this compelling book, meet in small group studies for a six-week period, and share personal insights with one another. We were blessed to have friends who invited Roger and me to join their small study group. Never having participated in a small study group, Roger was a bit hesitant, but to his credit he went with an open mind. What followed was six weeks of reading, learning, and sharing with ten individuals from whom I learned much about myself and my faith.

Why Is the Sky Blue?

I believe all of us at one time or other question why we are here.

Not only why we are here but why we experience the things we do? Why do some people seem to glide through life with little challenge or tragedy when others seem to be tested beyond imagination? The dichotomy reminds me of the "why is the sky blue?" question.

As Rick Warren points out, "The very experiences that you have resented or regretted most in life—the ones you've wanted to hide and forget—are the experiences God wants to use to help others" (p. 247). Who better to counsel a friend who just lost his job, than someone who had gone through the very same thing? I thought, "Who better to reach out to weary parents, baffled and defeated by their defiant child, than a mom who has lived it for years?"

He went on to say, "For God to use your painful experiences, you must be willing to share them. You have to stop covering them up, and you must honestly admit your faults, failures, and fears. People are always more encouraged when we share how God's grace helped us in weakness than when we brag about our own strengths" (p. 247).

Aldous Huxley said, "Experience is not what happens to you. It is what you do with what happens to you." So what was I going to do with my experiences? The answer was clear. You're holding it in your hands.

21

Making Sense of the Diagnosis

The day arrived for Roger and me to meet with Dr. Duane to review the results of the physiological studies, cognitive assessments, and psychological studies. With my file in hand, notes written down, and a prayer in my heart, I was ready for some answers.

Parent Consultation

With Ian still away, Dr. Duane agreed to meet with us. He usually prefers to have the patient present at the follow-up; however, he understood our sense of urgency. After several days of respite, we were better equipped to listen, question, and evaluate the information we'd receive. Dr. Duane began with a warm welcome and proceeded to share the results of the testing.

Results

We listened as he explained various laboratory results from blood work, including cholesterol, muscle enzyme, thyroid gland, pituitary gland, autoimmune profile, and serum lead levels. He addressed the findings of the routine electroencephalogram. In addition, Dr. Duane described how our son performed on auditory attention and memory, visual motor and visual perception skills, short-term and long-term memory, and attention assessments. Academically, reading, spelling, penmanship, and math were also evaluated.

The long parent forms I had resented filling out? We discussed the results of those as well. Parent Rating Scales, Achenbach Child Behavior Checklist, and the Children's Depression Index were all essential parts of the evaluation.

After discussing these findings, asking several questions, and taking pages of notes, we were there. There at the place we'd been traveling toward all along. In the office of a compassionate man experienced in treating children with defiance and their stressed-out families. There with a doctor who had provided a thorough neurological and behavioral examination. A doctor who was knowledgeable about our son's condition, who was knowledgeable about the best treatment (which included both medication and therapy), and on top of all that, who was compassionate.

So What Does It All Mean?

We now knew more about our son than we ever thought we would! But what did it all really mean? Dr. Duane had identified behaviors in Ian within minutes of talking with him and talking with us. Before he performed all the testing, I believe he already knew what we were dealing with. But after our years spent searching for answers, I knew that he would exhaust every possibility of any disorder before recommending treatment. That's why I knew we were in the right place.

After gathering and evaluating all the data, Dr. Duane had targeted the following areas of concern: aggression, obsessiveness, and depression. It was a vicious pattern of negative behavior. The good news? Dr. Duane recommended treating our son by adjusting his serotonin metabolism through medication. Dr. Duane had identified the underlying problems and set a course of treatment. We would begin with a low dosage in hopes that it would be sufficient. In seven days, Dr. Duane would call us to discuss the clinical response to the medications. In the months to follow, we would receive detailed progress reports any time we had concerns or if there were to be changes in Ian's treatment. The communication was vital to Ian's health and a great source of encouragement and support.

Steps Along the Journey

I found myself in the office of Dr. Natalie Schoenbauer, a highly regarded and knowledgeable school psychologist with the Scottsdale School District. I valued both her personal and professional opinions. I was meeting with her to discuss concerns I had with one of my students. In addition, I was asking for her feedback on a class assignment I had on oppositional defiant disorder (of all things). Standing there discussing students and class work, I couldn't hold back any longer. I had to discuss my own personal experience with my son. Not disclosing that I was struggling with a child with ODD would be tantamount to hiding something. It just wasn't right anymore. I was not going to be afraid to discuss it any longer. I asked her if she had a minute, and Dr. Schoenbauer and I proceeded to talk for the next twenty-five minutes. She gave me another precious gift that afternoon besides her time.

While she did not know Ian, I gave her a brief overview of his medical history and our family dynamics. Her undivided attention and encouragement allowed me to ask questions about the diagnosis, the treatment, and where it all fits in the area of education. All the while, I never felt as if I were being judged. Again, it was a freeing moment for me as a mom and as a professional educator. It was wonderful to openly discuss my son and not feel that familiar inner turmoil. Little by little I've stepped out in faith to open up and reach out to others. Each well-received conversation encourages me to continue to take those steps to let people in. I've come to realize that we really don't know the impact our words have on others or to what degree we affect their spirits. Parents with challenging children are oftentimes very fragile, exhausted, and confused. Meeting empathetic people on our paths truly makes the journey smoother.

Dr. Schoenbauer knew what questions to ask to get to the heart of the matter. Her first question was "What exactly was your son's diagnosis with the last neurologist?" Then "How has he been since he's been on the medication?" She went on to clarify that my son's oppositional defiance was a defense against his depression and obsessive compulsive disorder. In coping with these disorders, he had become hostile, angry, and defiant.

Dr. Harold S. Koplewicz, in his book, *More Than Moody*, discusses Kenny, a teenager who illustrates this behavior. "With teenagers with internalizing disorders, it's difficult but essential to find out what the adolescent is thinking and feeling to accurately diagnose him. In this case, Kenny's oppositional defiant behavior was a symptom of his depression and anxiety disorders" (p. 166).

As had Kenny, Ian had managed to hold it all together in school and sports but things were beginning to unravel for him. We were locked in a cycle of defiance, hostility, and anger. The aggression was brought on by intense feelings of being misunderstood. The obsessiveness was a defense against the disorganization of anxiety and depression. The anxiety was a precursor to the depression.

We had to treat the biological disorders before we could possibly make progress with behavior. As Dr. Duane pointed out, Ian was wired differently from the start. This was biological. We were unable to make any headway toward healing the behavior until the biological disorders were treated with the proper medication. While behavioral therapy may provide short-term results, in time it will all fall apart without the appropriate medication. That fact had been eluding us all along.

Just as authors Garbarino and Bedard point out in *Parents Under Siege* (2001) "Underneath the rude and obnoxious behavior may lie a highly sensitive child who is defending him or herself against being overwhelmed" (p. 137), we were raising a highly sensitive boy, who was indeed using defiant behavior as a defense mechanism. After years of frustration and despair, the defiant behavior was all he had left.

Dr. Schoenbauer went on to point out that it's been, in part, my personal experience that led me to the field of special education. She went on to discuss how many other educators in this field have some personal connection or story which gives them a heart for these special kids. That other gift she gave me? The gift of being listened to, valued, and affirmed.

Fast Forward

That initial consultation was over two years ago. In that time, Ian has been thriving under Dr. Duane's care. We continue to meet with him to monitor Ian's progress and adjust dosages as he grows. In addition, we communicate with our pediatrician and family physician with any concerns. We've discovered the boy who was in there all along, the boy who is funny, compassionate, and loving. This in turn, has completely altered the dynamics of our family. Over the course of time, we've begun to heal and move forward in our lives. We can plan, be more spontaneous, and participate in social activities again.

Laughter Is the Best Medicine

My family and friends noticed that I had become quite serious in recent years. I wonder why? Could it be exhaustion, disappointment, frustration, and fear? I hadn't found much to laugh about in my world. Looking back, it was about the time my Rescue Angels stepped in that I began to rediscover my sense of humor.

Along with the precious gift of time, my sisters gave me the gifts of encouragement, support, love and humor! They shared stories of fun things they did with Ian and funny interactions they all had with friends and family. With a little distance, I was able to see my son in a different light. I was also able to realize that I needed to take better care of myself physically, mentally, and spiritually.

The following year found me better able to cope by using this rediscovered sense of humor. All the pieces of the puzzle were beginning to fit together. Finally. The combination of the right care for Ian, respite care, family support, and my own treatment for situational depression brought those pieces together. I was able to laugh again, especially at myself. Recent trips and get-togethers with my sisters have been filled with the blessings of joy and laughter.

Ian has discovered his gift for making others laugh. In our family, he has become quite the entertainer. I'll be working in the study only to find him standing behind me saying "Luke, I am you *faaather*" a` la Darth Vader. Or, I'll be working in the kitchen and turn around to see him dancing with a colander on his head! I believe that, in his heart, Ian loves to make us laugh. Along with those I love yous the sound of sweet laughter in our home again is one of life's greatest gifts to me.

22

The Growing Season

A man's children and his garden both reflect the amount of weeding done during the growing season.

Unknown

new day had arrived in our household. Ian was now an eight-year-old boy on a hot summer day, with energy to burn. He found his dad in the study and asked, "Okay, Dad, can we play hockey in the garage now?" Keep in mind that an Arizona garage in June can easily reach over 120 degrees. Knowing this, my husband replied, "Let's throw the baseball in the yard instead." To which Ian responded, "But Dad, you promised to play hockey with me!"

It wasn't long ago that a situation such as this would have been the start of a slide down that slippery slope into defiance and meltdowns, leaving all of us exhausted daily. Instead, after weeks on new meds and under the care of a new doctor, the scene unfolded quite differently.

Roger had the courage to say "No, I didn't promise you I'd play hockey, but I will play catch with you." Ian walked away and dropped the idea of hockey. About a half hour later, standing in the family room, tossing a ball into his mitt, he said, "Okay, Dad, I'm ready to play catch. I'd really rather play hockey. But, okay."

This was such progress and growth. When I said Roger had the courage to say no to Ian, I used the word "courage" because, in the past, we would become locked in a pattern of manipulation. Roger had not promised hockey in the garage. Ian's plan of action was to manipulate Roger into thinking that he had. We were stuck in this destructive cycle. If we said no to our son's demands, we were guaranteed a meltdown and total defiance. As Ian got older, that defiance became abusive, both verbally and physically. If we said yes to his demands, we were resentful of being constantly manipulated by our child. We didn't enjoy the activity we were engaged in with him. It was an awful feeling, being controlled by our own child. Yet, this was the reality we were living with and it's the reality countless families today are living with.

At this stage of the journey, however, we were able to say no without the fear of total defiance. I look at this time as a period of growth and renewal in our family. We were adjusting to a more balanced life, learning new roles of behavior, and discovering healthy new boundaries. It's risky to open up your heart again if you fear the abuse returning. It becomes a day-to-day challenge. Because we were becoming stronger emotionally, physically, and spiritually, we were better equipped to meet that challenge head on.

All-star Moment

Upon returning from attending a seminar for the evening, my husband gave me some great news! Ian had shown concern for his dad's feelings in a big way. Roger had told Ian that he wanted the two of them to watch the All-Star baseball game together that evening: father-and-son time. Sometime during the fourth inning, Ian asked his dad if it would be okay to watch the game in the study where he could also play a computer game. The touching moment was found in the way he asked the question. "Dad, would you mind if I went into the study to watch the game? Would your feelings be hurt?" This from a boy who wasn't known for being sensitive to other people's feelings.

A Familiar Question

Along the way, each professional we visited had asked the same question: "Has your child ever harmed an animal?" Our reply was always the same: "No." In fact, it was because of the positive change in Ian when he was around dogs that we entertained the idea of getting a pet. The thought of a child intentionally harming an animal is disturbing; it conjures up images of cults and hideous, cruel behavior. What was the connection the professionals were looking for? I wanted to understand more.

On the website of The Humane Society of the United States, www.hsus.org, I found some answers. This informative site explores the connection between animal cruelty and human violence.

An article titled "Children and Animal Cruelty: What Parents Should Know" gave me some insights to the human-animal bond that in some cases has been threatened. There is definitely a connection between children's harming animals at a young age, and their becoming violent adults later in life.

Furthermore, statistics have shown that animal cruelty is perpetrated more often by boys than by girls. Children as young as four may abuse animals, but most incidents happen during the child's adolescence. The article explains, "If allowed to harm animals, children are more likely to be violent later in life. Animal cruelty, like any other violence, should never be attributed to a stage of development." There was the connection I had been looking for. Did Ian's behavior include harming animals? Was Ian's behavior crossing the boundary into cruelty to innocent animals?

It was a relevant question asked by each and every professional. Did my son ever harm animals? I'm thankful the answer was always the same: "No."

23

Learning What the Term "Pet Therapy" Really Means

God's hand continues to change my heart. Once a person who had no interest in dogs and pets in general, I've now become one of those "dog lovers." You know the type: the woman in the card shop looking over the dog figurines while her teenage daughter is rolling her eyes and giving the look.

If you had told me a year ago that I would be training a puppy this summer, I would have laughed at you! However, if I've learned one thing during this incredible journey we've been on, it's that life holds many surprises. I've changed in so many ways. Getting priorities in order and not sweating the small stuff is only the beginning. This outward change in me, the new dog lover, is evident to everyone who knows me. Ian had asked for a dog for quite a long time. The image of a boy and his dog comes to mind. Yet, with his challenges it was never a realistic option.

For one thing, I couldn't imagine drumming up any extra physical energy it would take to raise a puppy. As it was, I was exhausted from facing the daily demands of a child with ODD. And another concern was Ian himself. With all his rage, anger, and frustration, we weren't certain an innocent puppy wouldn't be the recipient of that rage. A scary thought for certain but then again we had all felt that uneasiness of threat in our own home.

I believed, once we started making progress, that a dog would bring out the compassionate side of Ian. However, Roger needed a little more convincing! I don't blame him; we had been through a lot of struggles and disappointments. Adding a new puppy to the family could possibly have been disastrous. He wanted to avoid any added heartache for our family. I understood his concern, yet I knew in my heart it would be a good thing. I'm happy to say it was one of our best decisions, and you'll soon understand why!

In *The Power of Pets*, Sally Abrahms explores the relationship between people and pets. She states, "The powerful connection between people and pets has been examined by physicians and scientists, and there are college programs that offer courses in animal-assisted therapy and animal-assisted activities, which are more recreational." Dogs are also introduced to lonely seniors, scared hospital patients, and even emotionally and physically abused and autistic children to achieve physical and psychological benefits.

In researching pet therapy, I discovered the world of Pets on Wheels. In fact, my own city has Pets on Wheels of Scottsdale, a nonprofit pet-visitation therapy program that serves sixteen health-care centers in Scottsdale. Up to 120 volunteers visit the elderly and/or infirm for an hour each week, bringing their dogs or cats. The benefits of pets in improving the quality of life for these individuals are discussed on the organization's website at www.petsonwheelsscottsdale.com. It states, "Studies show that pet visits provide warmth and affection for everyone involved, laughter, recollection of pleasant memories, mental stimulation for Alzheimer's patients, reduction in blood pressure, distraction from depression, lessening of tension and stress, reduction in incidence of heart attacks, comfort during periods of grief, motivation for therapy following injury or surgery, and a bright spot in the day—just being there."

At this writing, we've had Taffy, our beloved puppy, for six weeks. In that time, daily miracles and joy have abounded. I've seen the benefits of having a dog to love and care for. Not only has Taffy added a new dimension of fun to the household, she has given us all a healthy focus of growing, nurturing, responsibility, and most of all, compassion. Expressing compassion had always been a struggle for Ian. That was one of the areas that caused me the most concern. This puppy doesn't care what we look like; she just wants to love us. Taffy has brought out the very best in all of us and the days hold new joy because of her.

At this point, each day holds promise yet some days still fall short. Here is an excellent example of a day that fell short. It had all the ingredients for a meltdown: fatigue, hunger, and frustration. Upon being sent to his room for time in the penalty box, Ian asked if Taffy could come with him. My first gut response was to say no, but I quickly realized that this is what pet therapy is all about. Giving Ian a focus, in the form of a cuddly dog, was a benefit. Taffy would offer Ian the opportunity to reduce his level of stress by petting her, talking with her, and eventually working through his anger. Does the image of a boy in trouble, talking to his dog about things, come to mind? This was another one of our many breakthroughs along the way!

"Paws" to Reflect

The late Gilda Radner, in her book, *It's Always Something*, shared the following story of a friend's cousin's dog and I believe it fits in beautifully with our journey:

> When I was little, my nurse Dibby's cousin had a dog, just a mutt, and the dog was pregnant. I don't know how long dogs are pregnant, but she was due to have her puppies in about a week. She was out in the yard one day and got in the way of the lawn mower and her two hind legs got cut off. They rushed her to the vet and he said, "I can sew her up, or you can put her to sleep if you want, but the puppies are okay. She'll be able to deliver the puppies." Dibby's cousin said, "Keep her alive." So the vet sewed up her backside, and over the next week the dog learned to walk. She didn't spend any time worrying, she just learned to walk by taking two steps in the front and flipping up her backside, and then taking two steps and flipping up her backside again. She gave birth to six little

puppies, all in perfect health. She nursed them and
then weaned them. And when they learned to walk,
they all walked like her (p. 237).

I shared this moving story with Ian and we both smiled and
laughed. Then we talked about it further, reflecting on the real
message behind it. As parents, we possess an incredible—and oftentimes overwhelming—influence in our children's lives. Like these
sweet puppies, our children follow our lead, looking to us for direction. This reminds us that we must persevere with courage and faith,
no matter the challenges, for the sake of our children. What a beautiful example of overcoming obstacles, modeling behaviors, and
moving on with life.

"Paws" to Pray

As Taffy approached her six-month birthday, our veterinarian
recommended having her spayed. This added to the learning experience for all of us regarding the care and keeping of healthy dogs. Ian
had several good questions and wanted feedback about the procedure.
Beginning with our very first visit to the vet, Ian accompanied me
and participated in each visit. He was the one who answered the
doctor's questions, "How is Taffy eating? Is she playful? Is she drinking
lots of water?" With the upcoming procedure, I didn't want to him to
experience fear of the unknown and, consequently, more anxiety.
Children struggling with oppositional defiance are already coping
with more than their share of anxiety. Our veterinarian, Dr. Marilyn
Millman, was not only gifted with animals, she was gifted with children. She took Ian on a private tour of her offices, including the
surgery room where Taffy would be. When I mentioned that Ian may
be interested in becoming a veterinarian someday, Dr. Millman
offered to let him observe surgery sometime in the future. I've come
to appreciate kind people like this who truly make a difference in the
life of a child. If she only knew what the past several years have been

like for our family. Here she was giving us the gifts of kindness, compassion, and encouragement that our souls so desperately needed.

In my interview with Dr. Millman for this book, we shared conversation and insights into the world of pets and people, especially children. Dr. Millman has owned Animal Clinic Del Rancho in Scottsdale since 1994. In that time, she has developed a compelling interest in the problem of animal-welfare issues and pet overpopulation. This interest led to her founding of The Snip and Chip Foundation to promote sterilization and microchip identification. She also served on the board of the Arizona Humane Society for eight years. Her gentle spirit and love of animals are obvious to all who meet her.

She described the unconditional love that exists between animals and people, love that doesn't follow society's rules. Animals do not care what our social status is, what we look like, or even if we're grumpy. They love us unconditionally. Dr. Millman went on to say "We learn about tenderness in a way unlike any other" by caring for a pet. She described how the common goal of caring for a pet brings a family closer together. In fact, a few pets have been known to reside at the animal clinic for just this reason.

"While pet therapy benefits individuals and families, it is important to be certain the arrangement is good for the animal also," Dr. Millman stated. Parents need to be aware of the care and comfort of the pet. If a problem arises, a parent must intervene to keep that pet safe. Many times, situations that arise can be a good learning experience and all part of the responsibilities of owning a pet. Ultimately, adults need to be vigilant in keeping both pets and children safe.

I found one statement by Dr. Millman especially touching. We were talking again of the benefits of a pet for a child. She said, "Parents nurture kids. Who do the kids get to nurture?" She went on to say that children who care for and nurture a pet become invested in that pet. It's a winning combination and a healthy focus.

On the morning of Taffy's procedure, Ian was heading out the door to catch the bus to school. I assured him Taffy would be fine although I sensed his worry. I said, "Every time you feel anxious or scared today, say a prayer." Making it a word game, I said, "Let's 'paws' to pray! Dear God, please be with Taffy today, and bless Dr. Millman's hands and the technician's hands; please let them give Taffy compassion and lots of love." Instead of the usual reaction of the hand up and "Mom, stop it!" I heard this sweet whisper, "Okay Mom, I'll 'paws' to pray." This, compared to a mere six months ago, was real progress, a real blessing.

After taking Taffy to the vet, we went about our busy day. We received a phone call later in the afternoon, telling us the procedure had gone well. Taffy returned home quite groggy but fine. The relief on Ian's face was good to see, yet he continued to be anxious over her altered state. After explaining that it would be a couple of days before she would be her old self again, Ian started to relax. He was very gentle and attentive toward her.

The best part of this day happened during the precious minutes before bedtime. We said the usual bedtime prayers, and when I added, "And thank you, God, for taking good care of our precious puppy today," Ian said to me, "Mom, I prayed today."

In the days that followed, he treated Taffy with such love and compassion, I was overjoyed. My heart filled with love and thanks for the blessings that continued to pour forth with the addition of Taffy into our family. In fact, as of this writing, Leo, a sweet black and white puppy, has joined our household to keep Taffy company!

Without a doubt, the real gift that day was the sentence "Mom, I prayed today." Ian did indeed, "paws" to pray.

24

A Turkey in the Tenth Frame

O ur family was continuing to heal and learning to enjoy life again. Several months into his new medication plan, Ian was approaching his ninth birthday. We had seen a marked difference in our son. Activities once considered out of the question were now possibilities again.

For several weeks Ian and I enjoyed a tradition on Sunday mornings: bowling! Roger joined us on one occasion, but for the most part it was a mom-and-son thing. In the past, bowling was not an activity I would have chosen to participate in with my anger-ridden, on-the-edge boy. I could see it as it unfolded: high expectations for strikes and spares, competition to beat the other players, and frustration leading to rage when all did not go as planned. Thankfully, that was now in the past. It's a new day of hope and opportunity to do something as simple as bowling and enjoy it! Don't get me wrong, all is not perfect. In fact, the following story illustrates how far we've come and how each day continues to hold new challenges and victories.

Starting Off on the Right Foot

We learned to arrive by 9:30 in the morning to avoid having to wait for an open lane. On this particular day, we arrived on time and all went smoothly. Lane number twelve, size 4 1/2 kids' bowling shoes, ninety-nine cent bowling special, and we were on our way! First challenge, finding "Ian's" bowling ball. Not his own ball, mind you, but the bowling alley's ball. His favorite ball: orange, eight-pound, with a hairline crack above the left finger hole. Does that sound familiar? This would be where the obsessive-compulsive personality comes in.

While I was moving along, entering our names on the computer screen, putting my shoes on, and getting my ball, I was keenly aware that Ian was not finding his "orange, eight-pound, with a hairline crack above the left finger hole" ball. Problem number one. The morning was an especially busy one with lots of young families on both sides of our lane. Upon Ian's return to me, I miraculously spotted his ball on the very next lane. After I had encouraged him, he asked the teenager on that lane if he was using the orange ball. The boy replied, "No problem, go ahead take it." Phew! Problem number one solved. Unfortunately, there were many more problems ahead of us on that bowling Sunday.

Working Through It, Frame by Frame

Anyone who has bowled with young kids can bring to mind the image of a little one waddling up to the line, bowling ball in both hands, and plunk! The ball crawls down the glossy lane. Well, this describes the two young girls bowling next to our lane. While this is endearing to most, to a young boy with ODD, who has severe struggles with frustration levels and playing by the rules, it presented a perfect situation for a meltdown. However, at this point, Ian was much better equipped to handle everyday frustrations than previously. Much better, but not great at it! He certainly has his limit and it remains a bit lower than the average person's.

So now we had handled the ball problem and were aware that we were surrounded by younger children. Changing lanes wasn't an option, since the place was full. We realized we had to be patient with those around us. Next, as Ian threw the first ball of the first frame, he looked like he was stepping on ice: slipping all over the place! Okay! Now I had to solve this new problem. Using our computer intercom system, I called for the bowling attendant and kindly explained that we needed the lane wiped down, as it was very slippery. By now, the level was rising on Ian's frustration thermometer.

After the attendant wiped the lane down, I bowled. No problem. Next, Ian bowled and scowled as he slipped. This was not going well! We determined the shoes were the problem, so after changing shoes, presto! No more slipping!

Between the ball, the slippery shoes, the young, loud children, and the increasing noise level of the place, I could feel the tension building in him. I watched him grapple with his anger at what he saw as inconsiderate behavior by those around us. What he didn't understand, and I tried to point out to him, was that these little ones did not know bowling etiquette and didn't mean to throw off his game. Knowing I had to do something, I asked the mom next to me, "Excuse me, but my son is worried about your girls being so close as he bowls. He doesn't want to hit them with the ball. Could you have them walk back to the chairs after they have bowled? Thanks! And they're doing so well! They're really cute girls!" Here I was trying to teach bowling etiquette to a young mom busy with her own two little girls!

My job as the mom of a child with ODD has been, and will continue to be, part peace-keeper. In addition, I must be an advocate on his behalf. I've had to ask some people some pretty unusual questions. I had to present this request without offending the young mom. All the while, I could feel my own level of tension rising. But the interesting thing is, I've arrived at a place where I accept this as part of my job of parenting a challenging child. I don't have a normal situation. I have to speak up at difficult times when most kids could overlook some things. I have to ask some awkward questions and make some unusual requests. I will get strange reactions from other parents and onlookers who have little or no understanding of the situation we're in. As I looked around at all the families bowling, I wondered what challenges they have. So many dynamics were happening at lane number twelve!

As I had done so often in the past, I took deep breaths; overlooked Ian's frowns; said a silent prayer for strength, courage, and patience; and moved on. Toward the end of our first game, he was darting dirty looks to players on both sides of us and slouching in his chair. I continued to bowl pretty well, actually, all things considered! And this is where my special little guy amazed me. He perked up in his seat and said, "Great game Mom! I'll do better next game. The first is always a practice anyway. And I'll try not to be so mad." This is one of our victories! Victory over ODD running my son's life and the lives of his family. Victory over small frustrations adding up to insurmountable challenges. Sweet victory.

The Big Finish

Game two went much better and we found ourselves actually smiling at the situation. These moments gave me a glimpse at the mature side of my growing son. Toward the end of the third and last game, he just sat down until each side was finished with their boisterous bowling. It was a slower game for us, but one from which we grew.

At one point, he turned to me and said, "I keep having to wait," and rolled his eyes. Not in an angry way now, but in a way that said "You and I know these folks don't know bowling. It's not their fault, but I still don't like it." Almost like a secret that he was in on with me! The funniest moment came after the boy next to us made a strike. After all the yelling and jumping, while Ian was waiting to bowl, I said to him, "We have a lot to talk about in the car." Next thing I knew, the other boy reacted to his gutter ball by yelling "Boy, I suck this frame!" Wide-eyed, Ian said to me, "We have a lot more to talk about in the car, Mom." Great observations from a young boy!

Three Strikes and We're Outta There

During the course of this Sunday morning bowling, several little miracles took place. Beginning with not finding the bowling ball right away, maneuvering in slippery shoes, and lasting throughout a disruptive three games, something special happened. Ian and I took one problem at a time and worked through them together. He saw me patiently deal with each of those problems and took that as helping him out. It took every effort on my part to hang in there and stay positive.

In the past, I would have been quick to say "Let's go" and simply leave when the meltdown began. I cringe to imagine the scene that would have unfolded in our car on the way home. The rest of the day would have been ruined. Instead, this new reality we now live in gives me the strength to stick with the situation in the faith and hope that my son will work through his anger and manage his frustrations. The fact that Ian was actually able to smile at the situation (granted, not right away) and regain his composure was the real miracle that took place.

The fact that he was the one who turned it around, while I moved on with my game, is the real gift to me. I hold onto this as real growth and maturing on my son's part. I took the opportunity, between those boisterous bowlers, to tell Ian how very proud I was of him. I was proud of the way he handled the situation and needed to affirm his actions and attitude.

Oh, and the best bonus of the morning? For those readers who know a little bit about bowling, Ian bowled a "turkey" in the tenth frame (three strikes in a row) of our first game! And on top of that, in the third game, he earned his all-time highest score: 135! Yahoo! A great reward for Ian, who I believe really learned a lot about himself and his mom that morning.

A Winning Combination

Reflecting back on that Sunday morning, I realize what was involved in our triumph over the challenges presented. The first took place within me as a mom. It was because of the improvements in the months past that I was stronger in dealing with the problems before me. I wasn't in the dark place where exhaustion and fears held me captive. Until you are stronger physically, emotionally, and spiritually, you're not able as a parent to effectively deal with a challenging child. You're still in that "fight or flight" mode.

The second factor involved, obviously, was within Ian. This was clearly the first time he so effectively worked through not one but several frustrating situations. In the past, he would have looked at these as roadblocks he couldn't blast his way through. Anger would take hold and a rage would soon follow. It would actually follow us out of the bowling alley, into the car, and all the way home. Those of us who have lived that scenario know it well.

Changes in the mom and changes in the son, added up to a morning that ended successfully instead of sadly. It was, in the end, a good memory for a mom and her son. Oh, and let's not forget that turkey in the tenth frame too! Yes!

25

Dancing in the Dark

I've come to understand that life is made up of moments; some are ordinary and some are extraordinary. The day my son asked me to dance was an extraordinary moment. This wasn't just any dance; this was dancing in the dark. The dark garage.

It was a late afternoon in December. I was in the kitchen making a salad when Ian rushed in. "Mom, come here, please! Hurry!" He took my hand and I followed him through the laundry room to our attached garage. In the instant before he turned the lights off, I spotted his hockey net and stick, left where he had just been playing. On the opposite end of the garage two large orange construction cones marked the other goal. His boombox radio, perched on top of a large storage box, was playing one of our favorite songs, Matchbox Twenty's "Unwell" from the CD *More than You Know*. I couldn't help seeing the irony in this title after all we'd been through!

This popular song got a lot of play time on the local radio stations. Ian loved it! He held me close and started dancing with me! Right in the middle of our garage! In the dark! I couldn't stop thinking "Thank you God, for this moment! I want to freeze time. I want this song to play forever. What a precious, unbelievable, extraordinary moment!"

But like every moment, our time dancing in the dark came to an end. Ian simply said, "Okay, Mom." I hugged him and walked back into the house with a heart full of love and gratitude. Tucking him in that night, I said, "As long as I live, that time dancing in the garage with you will always be a favorite memory of mine. I love you."

Yes, life is made up of moments. Moments like these are what we need as parents of children struggling with defiance. They affirm our importance in our child's eyes. After all, we are human beings first; we have feelings. These moments help our love to grow. They give us glimpses into our children's hearts and memories to draw upon in challenging times. What a moment!

26
Follow the Signs

The process of writing this book has followed the same progression as Ian's journey: ups and downs, highs and lows. I would feel so inspired to get it down on paper that I would write for days at a time, only to stop writing for weeks at a time. In the early days, the goal was to get through the day. Going back to write about it was beyond my capability. By the time my children were asleep, I felt like a wet noodle. However, there were days when the need to write was almost physical and I felt inspired by the Holy Spirit. I believe all along I've had signs to keep at it, such as the following events that confirmed my calling to share this story.

Apples of Gold

Several months into my writing, I received an email from my sister Kathy. In conversation I had given her permission to share my story with others. I would soon realize how many families were struggling with defiant children. Not only is Kathy my personal Rescue Angel, she also happens to be an incredible inspiration to countless women and families in Michigan. Along with being a wife and a mom to three grown children, she is an inspirational speaker and writer. Through various ministries, including Moms in Touch and Apples of Gold, Kathy mentors women, inspiring them along the way. She is a prayer warrior who continued to lift my family in prayer during our darkest days. In addition, she single-handedly sent out a prayer request to fifty people to join her in praying me through the writing of this book.

Kathy knew a young mom experiencing frightening defiance in her son. While this mom was opening her heart to Kathy, my sister thought of our struggles. Knowing the other mom could use support, Kathy arranged for her to share her story with me via email. She made a plea for help which I knew from experience. I also recognized myself in her, as she stressed keeping the conversation private to protect her son. She had been seeking medical advice from pediatricians and was resisting medication options. She was looking for answers and instead found herself confused. She was on the same journey I had been traveling. Across the miles from one side of the country to the other, I felt her desperation and growing fatigue. She needed to connect with someone who could truly understand what she and her family were experiencing. We've since emailed each other several times, and I look forward to meeting her in person soon to share a hug and support.

Carson

This journey has brought people into my life I otherwise would never have met. Holly was such a person. I met Holly as I was finishing this book. Not including her inspiring story would have left a hole in this project. She shared her own unique journey of life with a challenging son and where it's brought her. We first met by phone and then communicated briefly by email. Finally, I had the pleasure of meeting her for coffee, which turned into two and a half hours of heartfelt conversation. She was open and honest as she poured out her story of a life filled with challenges and surprises. Through some tears and lots of laughter, we enjoyed sharing our similar stories and adventures in raising a challenging child. Like soldiers back from battle, we were able to affirm each other's victories and cry over our defeats. Best of all, we became fast friends who shared a common thread: we were parents who loved our children and were dedicated to being their advocates. We were on the path to healing and had much to share.

Seven-year-old Carson was Holly's only child, though he had the energy of about five children! During our first phone conversation Holly recounted the troubles Carson was having in school and at home. As a nurse, Holly was well versed in medical terms and conditions. Could this be ADHD? ODD? Is this more than simply a behavioral problem? She was at her wit's end. She and Carson's dad had divorced years prior; he now lived in another city. Holly was fortunate to have her mother living nearby; however, at age seventy, Grandma was becoming exhausted as she helped care for Carson. Holly knew she had to do something to change the course of little Carson's life.

School Daze

Holly began her story with Carson's experience in school. As parents we need the support of family and friends; in addition, we need the support of our child's school. In my case, I had built that beautiful red brick wall around Ian and our family, keeping his teachers out of the loop. In contrast, Holly was open and communicated her concerns and her son's needs to teachers and staff. Even in doing so, she struggled with some pretty awful experiences at the hand of one teacher in particular.

Holly described one school year in which she received a phone call from the office the first week of school. Carson was having a hard time adjusting to the new routine. A bright kid, he was struggling to perform in school while getting along with his peers. Things simply weren't fitting. At one point, Holly moved him from a public school into a private school. Hoping that a smaller classroom setting would give Carson more individualized attention, she found a local school and enrolled him. The results were disastrous.

Unfortunately, Carson had a teacher that was well past retirement age, well past having patience with challenging kids, and well past exercising good judgment in the classroom. While Holly's intentions were the best, the teacher was the worst. She was not only impatient and demeaning to Carson, at one point even hitting him in anger, she was committing a crime. Carson was injured, both physically and in spirit, the mom was enraged, the principal was horrified, and the teacher was fired. But, as most kids do, Carson bounced back. Upon seeing his old teacher in a store one day, he bounded up to her saying "hi," not seeming at all affected by her past mistakes, neither holding a grudge nor resentment.

The Teacher who Cared

At this point, Holly decided once again to enroll Carson in their neighborhood public school. Fortunately, this time Carson was blessed to have an excellent, sharp, compassionate teacher at the head of the classroom. In fact, it was this teacher who introduced me to Holly. She had had several parent conferences with Holly and knew Holly needed another parent to talk to, someone who had traveled the same tumultuous road Holly was now on. It was probably Holly's darkest time, and I was able to be a small glimmer of hope for her. If nothing else, I had been through a similar experience and I understood her distress. I was so grateful to have met her.

Something Brought you Here

After seeking help from pediatricians and family physicians, Holly decided to meet with a neurologist. After extensive testing, her son was diagnosed with obsessive compulsive disorder (OCD) along with some signs of ADHD. But the best thing she left with was the diagnosis. As in our case, rather than feeling discouragement with this diagnosis she felt a sense of relief and hope. There was a name to what her son was experiencing! How important having a diagnosis is.

Holly shared that even after a thorough examination by a respected neurologist, she still felt that tug of hesitation when deciding to use medication as a course of treatment. She and the doctor discussed the results of Carson's physiological studies, cognitive assessments, and psychological studies. After an hour-long discussion, Holly asked, "Do you really think we should use medication to treat Carson?" At which the doctor replied, "Something brought you here." With those words, Holly's eyes filled with tears as she recalled the struggles she had been through. Her questions were familiar: What is the best thing for my child? Am I taking the easy way out? Should I investigate more? How many tests, exams, and doctors do I need to see before I'm comfortable with my decision to use a prescription drug to treat my child?

As Holly explained, so many people are quick to judge our decisions when it comes to raising our children. Even within her own family, she had received harsh criticism. This, coming from a relative who only saw Carson occasionally! Being with our special kids once or twice a year is equivalent to viewing a large-canvas painting through a pinhole. In doing so, your view is distorted and you just don't see beauty of the whole picture. Yet these individuals feel they are able to comment on our choices as parents. Again, without having lived it, people simply cannot and should not judge our situation. I shared my own similar experiences with Holly. We agreed that this is where "building ourselves up" and advocating for our child comes in. I've discovered that I must surround myself with people who support me, who are empathetic to the situation, and who admit that they are not able to judge. In other words, we need all the help we can get.

A single parent, Holly had more than her share of responsibilities. She had a challenging child and a demanding sales career, and she was sinking fast. Something had to give. When we met, Holly had just sent Carson to visit his dad for a week. She had some precious respite time to reflect and rejuvenate. She had recently made the decision to quit her current job and work one day a week instead. She was blessed with the financial ability to do so, as well as the support of her nearby mom. In addition, she had decided to move forward in treating her son, as recommended by the neurologist, with medication. A new day was dawning for Holly and Carson. It was all coming together for them: an excellent doctor, a dedicated teacher, a supportive family, and a new job. I'll take the liberty to add one more: a kindred spirit and new friend in me! Seriously, I consider myself blessed to call Holly a friend. "Therefore encourage one another and build each other up, just as in fact, you are doing" (1 Thessalonians 11). This is what it's all about—building each other up and supporting one another through our challenges.

27

Class Conversations

During my coursework for special education, I have had the privilege of working with some very talented and inspiring instructors and fellow teachers. I recently completed a course in which the little-known topic of ODD was discussed. I say "little- known" because many in our class were unfamiliar with the term. One of the misconceptions was that ODD was part of ADHD. As pointed out earlier, while the two may co-exist, ODD and ADHD are separate disorders. The topic of medications and treatments were discussed. Behavior management techniques were discussed. All the while, I was a good listener and gave some general input regarding oppositional defiant characteristics. However, again I was guarded and didn't share that my own son has been struggling with this disorder.

Throughout my program, I worked with Mark Deal, a teacher with a master's degree in social studies who was now finishing his second master's in special education. His background included the field of criminal justice. He shared his story of working with Tyler, age ten, during a summer-school session at a local community center. He described Tyler as disruptive and defiant. He hadn't dealt with a child like this before and was at a loss for what strategies to use. Tyler would sit in the middle of a group activity and refuse to move. As games continued, he would not budge! He was angry, hostile toward others, and basically miserable. When it was time to walk to lunch, he would run ahead to the front of the line, pushing all the way. Mark had applied the usual strategies such as positive reinforcement (when he caught Tyler doing something good, which wasn't often enough), time-outs (which did not work), and communicating with Tyler to see if he could reach him (Tyler wasn't interested in talking). Mark truly wanted to reach this boy yet didn't know how.

Our group discussed the various behavior modifications that Mark had tried. As mentioned in a previous chapter, the use of positive reinforcements with an oppositional child tends to backfire. Public praise is seen by the child as an attempt by an authority figure to control. We know this is one of the main characteristics of oppositional defiance: the child will fiercely avoid being controlled by others. Knowing this, I commented in class that Mark may want to take Tyler aside and praise him without his peers noticing. The challenge, however, was in finding something to praise him for. He had isolated himself from the other children and most of the staff members didn't enjoy working with him. Tyler was caught in the grip of defiance.

In addition to the strategies given, the group agreed it would be helpful to talk with Tyler's parents. To his credit, Mark had already reviewed the file and discovered that the supervisor had met with the dad to discuss Tyler's behavior. Since the camp was run by a nonprofit organization, Mark had discovered parents were allowed to leave their children in the program providing there was no harm to the other campers. Mark walked away with little insight to help Tyler.

Mark appreciated the feedback and agreed it would be a challenge, but he was up for it. I thought I saw a shadow of doubt in his expression. Doubt or not, I admired his determination to help Tyler rather than simply to judge him as a lost cause. Mark realized Tyler had some serious problems and sincerely wanted to reach him.

During the discussion, I realized I was among a group of teachers who did not have a clear understanding of oppositional defiant disorder. In fact, the strategies and ideas they had would, in fact, exacerbate the situation. This is a common occurrence in classrooms today. Teachers who have thirty (or more) students are facing classroom- management challenges which include children with defiance. It is essential for teachers and staff to become familiar with the disorder, along with possible strategies to implement for coping with it.

After the course ended, I received an email from Mark stating that he was glad to be starting a new school year, but he had to admit, "I will miss Tyler. This was a real challenge. I wish I had longer to work with him." There's something about these kids that reaches our hearts. Tyler had reached Mark Deal's heart that summer.

Signs to share my story? These weren't just small signs; they were huge blinking neon signs.

I Am Not My Disability

Several individuals joined me in this journey—one of them was Mary Kramer, an instructor at the University of Phoenix. Mary had worked for ten years at Southwest Human Development serving children and families. When I met her, she was working in early intervention as a program manager and a disabilities training specialist. It was Mary who brought us to an off-site university meeting to tour the assistive technology department at Southwest Human Development. We were able to try out several pieces of adaptive equipment, from specially designed eating utensils to communication boards for individuals with speech impairment or severe communication difficulties. Mary encouraged hands-on experiences such as riding a special bike and recording voice messages. She explained that these devices gave individuals, from the very young to the elderly, more independence. We toured the offices and viewed the collection of large-print books and books-on-tape available to parents and families. It was a day of discovery and learning for our group of teachers.

After the assistive-technology tour, we were off to visit The Emily Center at Phoenix Children's Hospital. The Emily Center, located on the main floor of the hospital, is a library that is free and open to the public, offering materials about children's health, injuries and illnesses. It was founded by the Anderson family and named after their daughter Emily, who died from cancer at the age of seven. Their gift offers hope and support to countless individuals and families facing some of their darkest hours.

When we entered the library, it was soon obvious we were in a very special place. The atmosphere was one of comfort and welcome. It was a place for parents, families, and children to spend time searching for direction and answers, or sometimes just for peace and quiet from the busy activities of the hospital.

We discovered the wealth of information and resources available at The Emily Center. Each of us gravitated toward areas that interested us, as parents and as special education teachers. The materials were organized in a way that weary parents could find topics without necessarily having a medical background. Diseases were named in lay terms rather than medical terms. Nurses were available to help parents find materials they were looking for. Computers were also available with Internet access and health databases with full-text articles to review. Videos, cassettes, books-on-tape, and booklets filled the shelves!

In the section of children's books, I discovered books written for children facing a parent's terminal disease and death. Several books, in fact, were written for children facing either their own illness, the illness of a parent, or the illness of a family member. The books, illustrated with beautiful water-colors, addressed some of life's toughest challenges in words of hope, honesty, and encouragement. I took several books and spent time reading in a quiet, comfortable area. The library had such a sense of peace; it was a beacon of hope to so many. After class was dismissed I stayed behind on a big cozy couch, unaware of the time, reading books.

Mary was an instructor who truly wanted to make a difference by training successful teachers for today's classrooms. I know she made an impact on each one of us that day.

Mary brought a love for and dedication to special children into the classroom each day. She was the first to teach me to refer to a child not as a disability but as a child first. In other words, I don't teach autistic kids; I teach kids with autism. The little girl next door isn't the Down's syndrome girl; she is the girl with Down's syndrome. These are children, not disabilities.

Mary was also the first instructor with whom I shared my personal story. I had sensed her compassionate heart and felt safe disclosing my personal struggles. After class one morning, I asked to speak with her. She proceeded to listen and encourage me. I expressed how I had worked so hard at keeping the struggles private. I hadn't even shared it with my learning team, individuals with whom I had worked on a weekly basis over the past year. Then I added, "I've written the story of our journey. I haven't been able to talk about it, but I've written a book about it. A book by a parent for parents." She remarked that oftentimes the very best books on children with special needs are written by a parent.

It was Mary who first asked me "Nancy, what is it that you are afraid of?" That question silenced me. It stayed with me throughout the day. I'm glad she asked it. It gave me much to think about. What was I still afraid of?

It was in her class the next week that something miraculous happened. Our learning team had just finished giving a Power Point presentation on children with oppositional defiant disorder. I felt like a fraud in front of my fellow students. How could I keep this from the class? From my friends? It was time. Before I knew it, I looked over at Mary and said, "I'd like to add my personal experience to this presentation, Mary. May I have a few minutes?" First, a look of surprise then a soft whisper. "Are you sure, Nancy?" Yes. I was sure. I went on to share my story with the class. I tried to keep it simple, giving the highlights of the past several years. This is one of the reasons it had been so hard to talk about. Where to begin? I believe that's also one of the reasons I began to write about it. It was easier for me than talking about it just then. Their eyes were on me; I had their full attention. I started with a silent prayer, remembered the verse "Speak the truth in love" (Eph. 4:15), and felt an inner peace.

Afterwards, the room was quiet until one woman commented, "Thank you for sharing that." I felt such joy inside. Joy and relief. Mary told the class that I had confided in her and that it took great courage and a leap of faith to share that with the class. She went on to point out that here I was, an intelligent, active, concerned parent—and a teacher—and I too faced incredible obstacles. Disorders know no social or economic boundaries. I'll always be grateful for her gift of kindness and encouragement.

Recently, I attended a University of Phoenix class on other health impairments with Instructor Steven R. Isham, MA, CBSW. Steve is currently a special education teacher in Tolleson, Arizona, and works with students with emotional disabilities and mild mental retardation. His twenty-nine years of professional service to children and families throughout Arizona give him incredible insight into education and behavioral health. His list of accomplishments include serving as the executive director of Mentally Ill Kids In Distress (MIKID), a statewide private non-profit organization dedicated to assisting families with a child who has a mental illness or behavioral disorder in navigating the systems of children's behavioral health, education, juvenile justice, child protective services, and other systems of child and adolescent care. Steve also held the position of school principal of Far West in Buckeye, Arizona. He was responsible for this consortium school which served fourteen school districts to educate children with autism, mental retardation, emotional disabilities and severe multiple handicaps.

With his background, Steve brought time-tested and compassionate insights to the classroom. It was there that my heart for advocacy grew, and I was determined to reach out to parents through this book. He discussed the responsibilities we have as educators to keep the following key concepts in mind:

- *I am not my disability.*

- *Nothing about me without me.*

- *Physical limitation is not a mental disability.*

"I am not my disability" refers to what Mary Kramer had taught us, that the child is not the disability. Alicia is not an autistic girl, Alicia is a girl with autism. "Nothing about me without me" applies to the relationship between the parents, the child, and the school staff. A parent of a child with special needs does not need to enter a room filled with professionals and feel as if decisions regarding that child's education have all been made. Talk about intimidation! Finally, "Physical limitation is not a mental disability" means just that. A child with a physical challenge, perhaps confined to a wheelchair, can still be extremely intelligent. We cannot assume that, because of being in a wheelchair, a child is mentally challenged as well. These are three of many essential concepts for teachers, parents, and society to remember.

When I shared with Steve that I was writing this book, he was very enthusiastic. Once he recognized a fellow advocate for children and families, he gave me a CD entitled *"100" Positive Parent Affirmations,* presented by Amplitudes Audio Productions. As stated on the CD cover, "The 100 affirmations are designed to help parents become empowered by strengthening themselves and by keeping a perspective of their role as a parent in the process of advocating for their child and family."

Steve explained that the words and music are intended to offset the negative messages, either spoken or inferred, from the people and professionals who are dealing with your special child, the negative messages we receive from others while we're struggling with a defiant child in the store, the negative message when we hear the comment "You just need to be firmer in your discipline." All these things break our spirits. The CD is intended to build us back up and strengthen our families.

Listening to the CD, I felt myself relaxing and breathing. With soft background music, a gentle voice affirms, encourages, and builds up parents in the role of advocating for their children: "I am my child's best advocate. I know my child best. All children can learn; my child can learn. I am a good parent, and I can become a better parent." These are words we all need to hear as parents raising special children. In addition, the CD contains a listing of national parent and family resources and is included in the Parent Resource section at the back of this book.

Steve has dedicated his life to advocating on behalf of children and families. He, like Mary Kramer, was adamant about not defining a child by his or her disability. It is a lesson well learned and one that has stayed with me.

28

Victories

He was leaning over me as I was sleeping, cozy in my bed. "Mom, I need you to come into my room," Ian whispered as he limped away. I could hear him walking back toward his room, thump, thump, thump, down the long hallway. Slipping my feet into my fuzzy red winter slippers, I followed his path. He was in his bed, on his side, complaining that his right leg had shooting, throbbing pain. "Mom, it's killing me!" I looked at the time: 4:00. I sat on the side of the bed and calmed him by asking questions as I rubbed the leg. The first thing that came to mind was that he had slept on it and it had become numb. This was a logical conclusion. Knowing Ian had experienced "growing pains" in his feet (as diagnosed by our family physician), I wondered aloud if this could be the same thing. Not long ago, Ian had had problems with the heels of his feet. They were very painful when he put any pressure on them. After a week of warm-water foot baths and foot massages (which he of course loved) we took him to Dr. Carsia. After a thorough exam and even an X-ray to rule out any problem, Dr. Carsia determined that Ian was growing so quickly that the ligaments and tendons in his feet weren't keeping up. So there really is such a thing as growing pains! This was likely caused by the fact that Ian was a growing, healthy boy who experienced growth spurts that were unbelievable.

On this particular morning, I offered him Tylenol and watched as he took it with a large glass of cold water. I thought back to all the times we'd been up in the middle of the night with situations. That sense of urgency I referred to when Ian came into the world has stayed with us. The difference now, several years later, is that he has the ability to control his response to things. He has more patience, more understanding; he's simply more reasonable. Much of this comes from maturing I'm sure. But I'm convinced unless we found the right help for our son, that sense of urgency, coupled with oppositional defiance, would have had dire consequences for our son and for our entire family. The amazing thing is that I knew this all along the path.

Spoons

Here we were, at 4:00 in the morning. I asked, "Do you want to lie like spoons until you feel better?" We cuddled together, and I tried to take his mind off his sore muscles by talking about things. Within a few minutes, he began recalling the previous day when he had helped our neighbor work on his classic car.

Super Sport

Jim Nolton holds a mechanical engineering degree and recently earned a master of business administration (MBA). He has a real passion for mechanics and a real gift for teaching one young boy about classic cars. Jim lives down the street from us, and most days you can find him in his three-car garage working on one of his classic automobiles.

One sunny afternoon, Ian came running into the house in a whirlwind. "Mom! I'll be down at Jim's. I'm going to help him work on the Super Sport!" This was the beginning of a very special friendship. Jim was very patient and kind as he taught Ian, through hands-on experience, about cars. Ian even learned about an 8-track stereo! He explained it to me as "one of those things, about an inch thick and you put it into a box. It plays music." Jim even worked math lessons into their afternoons, teaching about fractions, as the sockets and open-end wrenches are labeled by fraction size. What special lessons in life and cars! What thankful people we were to have Jim Nolton as our neighbor.

Recently, Ian spent the afternoon working on and learning all about a 1971 Chevelle Super Sport. This was one of two classic cars Jim was restoring. On this day, Ian learned first hand what the engine looks like from underneath the car! Rolling under the car, on a "Creepy Crawler," Ian got a good look at the underside of this beautiful red classic car.

Here we were now, before dawn, talking cars. I loved hearing him recall the steps of replacing a chrome bumper and telling me how the exhaust system works. He went on to explain how the engine gets hot and the fumes go out through the exhaust pipe, which Ian described as "a squiggly pipe underneath the car." He said, "I can't remember what those things are called that pump up and down." When I said, "Oh, do you mean the pistons?" his astonishment brought a smile to my face. "How did you know that Mom?"

I explained that I always like to surprise him when, in fact, I was blessed with a dad who also had a Super Sport—a 1967 Chevy Camaro, which he had restored. A white convertible with red pin striping, red leather interior, and sparkling wire wheel covers, it was a beauty. Some of my favorite childhood memories are of being alongside my dad as he worked on that beautiful Camaro. Not only did we share conversation in the driveway, we shared some of life's greatest lessons: patience, perseverance, learning, and love. I was his assistant as he checked the oil, replaced filters, and greased bearings. I even accompanied him to the auto parts store whenever he needed that certain part. I can still visualize the man behind the counter flipping through page after page of a catalog, searching for just the right part. It was a real adventure to this young girl. Our time together will always hold a very special place in my heart.

Someday Ian will look back at those memories of time spent with Jim and his classic cars and see time spent learning some of life's greatest lessons.

29

The Joy of Peace

The most inspiring victories include moments with Abby and Ian. After one particularly long day when Ian was resting with an ear infection, we had one of those victories.

I had stayed home with Ian and we enjoyed a quiet day together. The calm before the storm! Now it was the busy hour at our house. Abby and Roger were returning from school and work, dinner was cooking on the stove, the dogs were barking, and Abby was planning an evening out to watch a high school basketball game. The doorbell rang. As I looked out the window, I saw our little red-headed, eight-year-old neighbor, dressed in her Girl Scout uniform complete with decorated sash, holding the familiar Girl Scout cookie order form. Would we like to order cookies? Of course we would! Does this scene sound familiar? It plays out across the country every day! We have such busy households.

Amidst all the commotion, Ian was asking for grapes. I replied, "Ian, we're out of grapes. I'll buy some tomorrow at the grocery store. Promise." Well, this answer was not what he wanted to hear. Not feeling well and becoming more and more restless, he wouldn't drop it. He really wanted those grapes! In the past, something this simple could send him into a rage, especially when he wasn't feeling well. This time, he was more reasonable and better able to handle disappointment. He still let me know that he *really* wanted some grapes. I was thankful that I didn't hear more about it as I finished preparing dinner and we began to eat our meal.

After the dishes were cleared, Abby headed out the door with a quick kiss good-bye. Ian and Roger settled into the couches to enjoy a basketball game on TV. The quiet after the storm! Just as I sat down to check my email, the doorbell rang again! Taffy and Leo started barking. Ian ran to the door, and I looked out to see a dark, empty courtyard. Cautiously, I opened the door to find a bag on the mat. At the same time, I heard a car heading down the street. Ian and I opened the bag to find a bunch of fresh green grapes! Abby had stopped at the store to buy her brother his much-desired grapes before going to the game. It was completely spontaneous, not asked for, and incredibly appreciated! These are what I refer to as "victories." What Abby did was an act of kindness toward her brother and a heart-warming gift to our entire family. What would be considered a small gesture for many, was an incredible display of love, healing, and hope for a family who had been through so many challenges. Sweet grapes. Sweet victory.

TO PEACE!
By Ian Hagener
Elementary School
2003

Peace is a great thing to have in
the United States.
We are lucky to have cars, friends,
and the most important thing is family.
If we didn't have peace, the world would
be a disaster!
We wouldn't be able to play outside
and have a good life.

30

Reflections

While taking a class on emotional disorders, I found myself listening to lectures on the very life we'd been living. After the first session, I approached my instructor, who was knowledgeable, compassionate, and enthusiastic. She too had a loved one in her family coping with a disability. This gave her that wonderful trait called insight. In our conversation, she listened and asked me some key questions. Her questions have stayed with me since then. Looking at me with kindness she asked, "Why are you afraid to talk about it with others? What is it that scares you?"

As parents of children with special needs, we know that those types of questions are complicated. Why was I afraid? Was I being protective of my son? Was I afraid of his being labeled? Was I protecting my daughter? My family? Did I feel like a failure? The answer to all of the above is "yes." In reflecting on my instructor's questions, I also realize another aspect of this whole sharing process: fatigue. It takes energy to open up the dialogue of life with ODD, energy I've been very short of in the past several years.

In addition, I now see that when I'm in my role at work or school I don't have to be the mom of a challenging child. I can just be myself, as a teacher and student who loves her work. Bringing all the other information in, disclosing the struggles, would bring it into my place of work; it would be part of every aspect of my life. I needed to have something separate from the challenges. Parents need to recharge and have a break from focusing on their special child. I compartmentalized my life to the extreme. It had been my way of coping. Finding a healthy balance was the key. Every one of us is different and needs to find our own way.

It's been interesting to see life unfold for our family. That sweet daughter I've discussed? Abby is now a compassionate young woman, working with children. That little girl who, on Valentine's Day so many years ago, was thrilled at the thought of having a baby brother? Her heart has been through some pretty rough spots in which she has shown me the depth of her soul. Her love and patience, sense of humor and joy, have taught me so many valuable life lessons. The years have shaped the woman she will become. I believe God has been growing her for great works.

Oh, the joy I see in my husband and son sharing their love of sports! I am so grateful that Ian has been blessed with athletic ability, something on which we can help him focus and build in a healthy way. In the earlier days, sports were an obsession, in some cases leading to full-blown tantrums. Lost soccer games brought out the worst in Ian, resulting in physical aggression toward us. It was a vicious cycle: we wanted him to be involved in sports as a healthy way to run off some energy, but if the results of the game were bad, it was all over. Images of Roger, exhausted as he came home after a game or practice, with Ian yelling and punching the walls, come to mind. To his credit, Roger never gave up. Through years of soccer, hockey, golf, and baseball, he encouraged our son. Always one for quality equipment, Roger outfitted Ian with the best sports gear. Believing in the benefit of lessons, he signed Ian up for the batting cages, pitching lessons, and sports camps. He taught Ian the love of the game, good sportsmanship, and above all, how very much his dad loved him.

Life has taken incredible turns for our family. There are times I look back and I am amazed at the changes in my child. Moreover, I am amazed at the changes in myself as a mother and a woman. This journey has so completely changed me that I've begun to redefine my goals, attitudes, and outlook on life. The joy in this is that I can actually give myself the gift of setting goals for myself other than surviving the next hour or the next day. And furthermore, my son is happy and

I can see him growing into a compassionate, albeit still intense, young man.

There have been some inspiring moments in our lives this past year, namely, discovering who my son actually is underneath all the anger, obsessions, and defiance. There is such reward in seeing happiness on his face. His delightful sense of humor and outlook make us laugh. Each day he is growing more compassionate, understanding, and helpful. The goal of my children loving each other? They always have; the best part is now they show it. In fact, I believe they will have a special bond throughout their lives because they've been through such challenging times together.

I will never take an "I love you, Mom," for granted. I will never pass up an opportunity for a hug, a kiss, or even a touch of affection from my son. Many years went by without any of these gifts. I didn't realize how very much I ached for this contact with him until we finally had a breakthrough and I saw a gentler side of him. I began letting him back into my heart. I had been so angry with him for the chaos he brought to our family. Oftentimes I didn't want to be near him, and looking back, I realize he sensed that. What a sad situation.

Oppositional defiant disorder is one of the most challenging disorders to identify and treat. It's oftentimes coupled with other existing conditions, making it part of a difficult puzzle. In the process, marriages and families are daily put under incredible stress and trials. Left untreated, ODD may lead to conduct disorder and eventually destroy both the child and the family members. The stakes are extremely high. We must not give up on our special children. We must be their fiercest advocates.

In my heart, I believe this experience was all part of God's master plan for me. Throughout this journey, He has shaped me for a purpose. Through God's leading and gentle nudging, I was able to write this book. Furthermore, at the start of my writing I faced the decision of working in the field of special education as an instructional assistant. I was concerned that working with special children and coming home to my own children might put me over the edge. It did just the opposite. Working with these kids has given me such joy.

This joy led me to further my education and to become a special education teacher, a career I had not considered previously but one that is a perfect fit.

Only because Ian got the help he needed, and our family began to heal, was this opportunity even a possibility. Going to graduate school, teaching in my own classroom, and stepping out in faith have been incredible gifts to me. I believe the past ten years of experience have brought me to this place. I am thankful for the blessing that is my son and for the ways in which we all have grown.

My goal in writing this book was to give parents hope and encouragement as they face the task of raising a child who is defiant. The journey doesn't end here, though. It continues as a lifelong process. We are grateful that, for our family, it's better traveling these days. My prayer for you is better traveling as well.

Thoughts for the Continued Journey

If you take anything away from reading this book, I hope it includes the following thoughts. It takes a team of caring individuals, dedicated to treating the child and the entire family unit, to find the right combination of treatment. Once found, the combination will change as the child grows. It was this successful combination of medication and therapy that brought us to a good place.

Our journey was a long one during which we were at times desperately seeking help from a variety of professionals. We started with our first pediatrician when our son was born. From there, we saw two pediatricians, family physicians, a family therapist, a neuropsychologist, a neurologist, a clinical psychologist, a school psychologist and school teachers. We experienced a myriad of emotions: vulnerability, fear, anxiety, and anger. We did not always know what to ask or whom to trust. We simply knew we had to keep searching for direction.

I've learned in my attempts that it is essential to start by working with a trusted pediatrician to rule out any medical problems the child may have. Each child is biologically unique, and many have more than one condition that needs to be addressed. When we first used medication to treat my son's ODD, I thought of it as a miracle pill. I've since learned there is no such thing. No one pill will be the answer. I've also learned that many pediatricians shy away from treating children with disorders such as ODD, ADHD, and depression. That's why it is so important to find a pediatrician who has a heart for children and families, who is progressive in treating children with medication when needed, who is flexible in trying different types of medications, and who is an active member of your support team. As parents we need to seek out these professionals and work together toward solutions.

Furthermore, I've learned that with a proper diagnosis, medication can be the start of healing. The proper medication gives the severely distressed child the gift of relief. As my son put it, to "not be mean anymore." These kids are miserable, exhausted, and misunderstood. Once the medication has had a therapeutic effect, the child who was once angry, defiant, and hostile becomes more reasonable and begins to feel better. Each child is an individual and each case must be evaluated as such. It is necessary to address the underlying medical problems before we can make any headway with therapy. This brings me back to the team of support.

I've seen incredible, positive changes in my son with the help of medication coupled with therapy. He has had the opportunity to feel better and actually *appreciates* when he feels good. He is able to communicate how he feels and discuss how the medication has helped him. A far cry from the days of sneaking the medication into the ice cream.

However, our struggles and challenges are not over. Treatment must be on-going, with regular visits with the team—pediatricians, family doctors, neurologists, therapists, and teachers. It's also essential for the team to communicate with one another on treatment and progress. The idea isn't to revisit our past issues, but to resolve them, make peace, and move on with life.

Parent and Family Resource Guide

Suggested Readings

American Psychiatric Association: *Diagnostic and Statistical Manual of Mental Disorders,* Fourth Edition, Text Revision. Washington, DC, American Psychiatric Association, 2000.

Dobson, Dr. James *The New Strong-Willed Child.* Wheaton, IL: Tyndale House Publishers, Inc., 2004.

Garbarino, James & Bedard, Clarie *Parents Under Siege: Why You are the Solution, not the Problem, in your Child's Life.* New York: The Free Press, 2001.

Green, Dr. Ross W. *The Explosive Child.* New York: HarperCollins, 2001.

Koplewicz, Dr. Harold S. *More than Moody: Recognizing and Treating Adolescent Depression.* New York: Penguin Books, 2002.

Radner, Gilda. *It's Always Something.* New York: HarperCollins, 1989.

Riley, Dr. Douglas A. *The Defiant Child: A Parent's Guide to Oppositional Defiant Disorder.* Maryland: Taylor Trade Publishing, 1997.

Taylor, John F. *From Defiance to Cooperation: Real Solutions for Transforming the Angry, Defiant, Discouraged Child.* New York: Three Rivers Press, 2001.

Wilens, Dr. Timothy E. Straight *Talk about Psychiatric Medications for Kids.* New York: The Guilford Press, 2001.

Nancy A. Hagener

CD & Print Resource

"100" Positive Parent Affirmations, presented by Amplitudes Audio
Productions,
PO Box 236,
Tolleson, AZ 85353.

You Can Handle Them All Quick-Action Card Deck (1992)
The Master Teacher
Leadership Lane
PO Box 1207
Manhattan, Kansas 66505-1207
(800) 669-9633
Web: www.masterteacher.com

National Organizations

Children and Adults with Attention-Deficit/Hyperactivity Disorder
(CHADD)
8181 Professional Place, Suite 150
Landover, MD 20785
(800) 233-4050
(301) 306-7070
(301) 306-7090-Fax
Web: www.chad.org
The nation's leading non-profit organization serving individuals
with ADD/ADHD through advocacy, research, education, and
support to parents, educators, and the general public.

Council for Exceptional Children
1110 North Glebe Road, Suite 300
Arlington, VA 22201-5704
(888) CEC-SPED-Toll Free
(703) 620-3660-Local
(866) 915-5000-TTY, (text only)

(703) 264-9494-Fax
Web: www.cec.sped.org
The largest international professional organization dedicated to improving educational outcomes for individuals with exceptionalities, students with disabilities, and/or the gifted. Helps parents and families by providing information on special education laws, advocacy, and resources available.

Federation for Children with Special Needs
1135 Tremont Street, Suite 420
Boston, MA 02120
(617) 236-7210
(800) 331-0688 (in MA)
(617) 572-2094-Fax
Web: www.fcsn.org
Over thirty years of parents helping parents; offers a variety of services to parents and individuals working with children with special needs.

National Information Center for Children and Youth with Disabilities (NICHCY)
PO Box 1492
Washington, DC 20013
(800) 695-0285-V/TTY
(202) 884-8441-Fax
Web: www.nichcy.org
Funded by the Office of Special Education Programs (OSEP) at the U.S. Department of Education, provides resources to parents and families of children with disabilities; includes information on Individuals with Disabilities Act (IDEA), No Child Left Behind (NCLB), and research-based information on education practices.

Nancy A. Hagener

National Institute of Mental Health
    6001 Executive Blvd., Room 8184, MSC 9663
    Bethesda, MD 20892-9663
    (301) 443-4513-Local
    (301) 443-8431-TTY
    1-866-615-6464-Toll Free
    Web: www.nimh.nih.gov
    National Institute of Mental Health is the lead Federal agency
    for research on mental and behavioral disorders.

Parents Anonymous, Inc.
    675 West Foothill Blvd., Suite 220
    Claremont, CA 91711-3475
    (909) 621-6184
    (909) 625-6304-Fax
    Web: www.parentsanonymous.org
    The nation's oldest child abuse prevention organization, dedi-
    cated to strengthening families and building caring
    communities that support safe and nurturing homes for all
    children.

The American Academy of Pediatrics (AAP)
    National Headquarters
    141 Northwest Point Boulevard
    Elk Grove Village, IL 60007-1098
    (847) 434-4000
    (847) 434-8000-Fax
    Web: www.aap.org
    Official website of the AAP, an organization of 60,000 pediatri-
    cians committed to the physical, mental, and social health and
    well-being of infants, children, adolescents and young adults.

The ARC of the United States
    National Headquarters
    1010 Wayne Avenue, Suite 650
    Silver Spring, MD 20910
    (301) 565-3842
    (301) 565-3843-Fax
    Web: www.thearc.org
    Founded in 1950; works to include all children and adults with
    cognitive and developmental disabilities in every community.

Websites

American Academy of Child and Adolescent Psychiatry
    www.aacap.org/publications/factsfam
    The American Academy of Child and Adolescent Psychiatry
    developed Facts for Families, which provides information on
    issues that affect children, teenagers, and their families.
    Includes information on over 70 disorders, including opposi-
    tional defiant disorder.

ARCH National Respite Network and Resource Center
    www.respitelocator.org/index.htm
    Respite locator for parents and caregivers of children and
    seniors. Listed by state and local areas to match specific needs
    of individuals. Organizations listed by name include phone
    numbers, and in many cases, website addresses. Many services
    include family resource programs, behavioral health services,
    parenting classes, and child activities.

Band-Aides and Blackboards
    www.funrsc.fairfield.edu/~jfleitas/contents.html
    Provides resources for those growing up with illness or disabili-
    ties and their families. Includes information for children, teens,
    and adults. Excellent resource for siblings; includes shared
    stories and sibling support.

ConductDisorders.com
    www.conductdisorders.com
    website developed by parents raising challenging children,
    oppositional and resistant to parenting; describes as its goal to
    be a "soft place to land for the battle-weary parent;" resources
    include parent forums, articles, books, and helpful feature links.

Mental-Health-Matters.com
    www.mental-health-matters.com
    Provides information about mental health issues, offering
    details on disorders, symptoms, and treatment modes to help
    educate consumers. Current articles featuring ODD, CD, and
    ADD/ADHD.

National Parent Information Network
    www.npin.org/about.html
    Sponsored by the U.S. Department of Education, provides
    resources on education, parenting, child care, and child devel-
    opment.

Not MY Kid, Inc.
    www.notmykid.org
    Dedicated to raising awareness about the most prevalent youth
    and adolescent mental and behavioral health issues.

PACER Center
    www.pacer.org/ebd
    Provides resources for parents and families who wish to improve
    their advocacy skills or who require information and assistance
    in accessing services for their children with emotional or
    behavioral disorders.

Parents and Teachers of Explosive Kids (P.T.E.K.)
    www.explosivekids.org
    A parent-driven, nonprofit organization providing education

and support for parents and teachers involved in the care of behaviorally challenging children. Includes resources, message board, and updates from Dr. Ross Greene, author of *The Explosive Child*.

The Emily Center at Phoenix Children's Hospital
1919 E. Thomas Road
Phoenix, AZ 85016
(602) 546-1400
E-mail: emilyc@phoenixchildrens.com
Web: www.phxchildrens.com/about/services/emilycenter
A nonprofit community service. Library and nurse assistance in research available to residents of Arizona. Completely supported by donations and fundraising dollars.

US Department of Education
www.ed.gov
Provides A-Z listing of topics addressing education in the United States. Information on laws relating to IDEA and No Child Left Behind among others.

Yellow Pages for Kids with Disabilities
www.yellowpagesforkids.com
Provides listing of resource contacts, including advocates, government programs, and parent support groups.

While the author has made every effort to provide accurate telephone numbers and Internet addresses at the time of publication, neither the publisher nor the author assumes any responsibilities for errors or for changes that occur after publication.

Glossary

advocate: A person who speaks or writes in support or defense of another person; a method parents of students with disabilities can use to obtain needed or improved services.

aggression: Behavior that intentionally causes others harm or that elicits escape or avoidance responses from others.

antidepressants: Medications used to treat unipolar mood disorders (depression). They include three specific types: selective serotonin reuptake inhibitors (SSRIs), monoamineoxidase inhibitors (MAOIs), and tricyclic antidepressants.

anxiety disorder: A disorder characterized by anxiety, fearfulness, and avoidance of ordinary activities because of anxiety or fear.

attention deficit hyperactivity disorder (ADHD): A condition characterized by severe problems of inattention, hyperactivity, and/or impulsivity; often found in persons with learning disabilities.

behavior management: Strategies and techniques used to increase desirable behavior and decrease undesirable behavior. May be applied in the classroom, home, or other environment.

behavioral: Focusing on behavior itself and the observable conditions and events causing it, rather than unconscious motivations.

bipolar disorder: A mood disorder characterized by varying episodes of highs (mania) or lows (hypomania) and depression.

cognitive: Related to thinking or knowing.

collaborative consultation: An approach in which a special educator and a general educator work together to come up with teaching strategies for a student with disabilities. The relationship between medical professionals, parents, teachers, and individuals based on the premises of shared responsibility and equal authority.

comorbidity: Co-occurrence of two or more conditions in the same individual.

conduct disorder: A disorder characterized by overt, aggressive, disruptive behavior or covert antisocial acts such as stealing, lying, and fire setting; may include both overt and covert acts.

criteria: Standards by which something may be judged.

defiance: A daring or bold resistance to authority with open disregard; contempt.

depression: A mental state of depressed mood characterized by feelings of sadness, despair, loss of interest, and loss of enjoyment in life.

developmental: Pertaining to the process of growth and differentiation.

externalizing: Acting-out behavior; aggressive or disruptive behavior that is observable as behavior directed toward others.

indirect reinforcement: Finding ways to discreetly support the desirable behavior of an individual rather than punishing the undesirable behavior; a nod of the head, a whisper of praise.

individualized education plan (IEP): IDEA requires an IEP to be drawn up by the educational team for each exceptional child; the IEP must include a statement of present educational performance, instructional goals, educational services to be provided, and criteria and procedures for determining that the instructional objectives are being met.

Individuals with Disabilities Education Act (IDEA): The Individuals with Disabilities Education Act of 1990 and its amendments of 1997; replaced PL 94-142. A federal law stating that to receive funds under the act, every school system in the nation must provide a free, appropriate public education for every child between the ages of three and twenty-one, regardless of how or how seriously he or she may be disabled.

internalizing: Acting-in behavior; anxiety, fearfulness, withdrawal, and other indications of an individual's mood or internal state.

major depressive disorder (MDD): A serious depression lasting six months or longer. Has many similarities in both adults and adolescents: sadness, pessimism, sleep and appetite disturbances, and decreased concentration and sex drive. In adolescents, these symptoms can also be accompanied by anxiety and irritability.

neurologist: A physician whose practice focuses on the diagnosis and treatment of disorders of the nervous system.

neuropsychology: a discipline combining neurology and psychology.

obsessive-compulsive disorder: Recurrent obsessions or repetitive behaviors (such as hand washing) or mental acts (such as counting, repeating words silently) that are severe enough to be time consuming or cause marked distress or significant impairment.

oppositional defiant disorder: A disorder characterized by a recurrent pattern of negativistic, defiant, disobedient, and hostile behavior toward authority figures that persists for at least 6 months.

pharmacotherapy: The treatment of a condition using medications.

physiological: Pertaining to the branch of science which treats the functions of living organisms and their parts, including all physical and chemical processes.

psychological: Pertaining to the branch of science which deals with the mind and mental processes, especially in relation to human and animal behavior.

positive reinforcement: Finding ways to support the desirable behavior of an individual rather than punishing the undesirable behavior.

temperament: A character trait an infant is born with; sometimes thought of as a child's inherent disposition and the foundation of their personality.

tolerance: The loss of a response, either behavioral or physical, to a medication over a sustained period of time.

Bibliography

Abrahms, S. *The Power of Pets.* Retrieved February 1, 2005, from www.holisticonline.com/pettherapy.

American Psychiatric Association: *Diagnostic and Statistical Manual of Mental Health Disorders,* Fourth Edition, Text Revision. Washington, DC, American Psychiatric Association, 2000.

American Academy of Pediatrics. *Understanding ADHD: Information for Parents About Attention Deficit/Hyperactivity Disorder,* 2001.

Band-Aides and Blackboards. *Love Me, Love Me Not.* (2004, November 14). Retrieved January 20, 2005, from http://funrsc.fairfield.edu/~jfleitas/contents.html

Connelly, E. R. *The Encyclopedia of Psychological Disorders: Sibling Rivalry.* Philadelphia: Chelsea House Publishers, 2000.

DeBruyn, R. L. and Larson, J. L. *You Can Handle Them All Quick-Action Card Deck.* Manhattan, Kansas: The Master Teacher, Inc. 1992.

Dobson, James. *The New Strong-Willed Child.* Wheaton: Tyndale House Publishers, 2004.

Doerper, J. *Wine Country: California's Napa & Sonoma Valleys.* Oakland: Compass American Guides, 2000.

Garbarino, J. and Bedard, C. *Parents Under Siege: Why You are the Solution, Not the Problem in your Child's Life.* New York: The Free Press, 2001.

Green, Ross W. *The Explosive Child.* New York: Harper Collins, 2001.

Hallahan, Daniel P. and Kauffman, James M. *Exceptional Learners:*

Introduction to Special Education. 9th ed. Boston: Pearson Education, Inc., 2003.

Humane Society of the United States. www.hsus.org

Kingsley, Emily Perl. "Welcome to Holland" 1987.

Koplewicz, Harold S. *More than Moody: Recognizing and Treating Adolescent Depression.* New York: The Berkley Publishing Group, 2002.

Matchbox Twenty, *More than you think you know,* compact disc, Bidnis, Inc./EMI, Blackwood Music, Inc. (BMI), 2002.

Radner, Gilda. *It's Always Something.* New York: Harper Collins, 2000.

Riley, Douglas. *The Defiant Child: A Parent's Guide to Oppositional Defiant Disorder.* Maryland: Taylor Trade Publishing, 1997.

Santa Maria, Karen. Arizona Department of Education (ADE). *Glossary of Special Education Terms.* (2001)

Spratto, George R. and Woods, Adrienne L. *2005 Edition PDR Nurse's Drug Handbook.* New York: Thomson Delmar Learning, 2005.

Warren, Rick. *The Purpose Driven Life: What on Earth are We Here For?* Grand Rapids: Zondervan Press, 2002.

"100" Positive parent Affirmations, compact disc, Amplitudes Audio Productions, 2003.

Index

G

grieving process, 27
growing pains, 177

I

IDEA, 47-48
Individuals With Disabilities
 Act. *See* IDEA
illustrations, 60, 183
Isham, Steven R. (university
 instructor), 174-176
isolation, 19-21, 23, 25-26, 36,
 40, 66, 81, 83, 88, 90, 92-93,
 97-98, 102, 113, 185-186

K

Kramer, Mary (university
 instructor), 171, 172-174

L

LD, 45
learning disabilities. See LD

M

marriage, stresses on, 20, 31-32,
 36, 53-55, 66. 75, 76, 78, 97
Martig, Roger M. (clinical
 psychologist), 29-37
Millman, Marilyn (veteri-
 narian), 152-154

N

neuropsychology, pediatric, 37-
 38
  evaluation assessments, 38
  tests, 39, 40

O

obsessive compulsive disorder.
 See OCD
OCD, 92, 93, 94, 166
ODD, 92-93
  behavioral therapy, 31, 34-35,
  59
    holding method (therapy),
    18-21
    indirect reinforcement, 49
    play therapy, 30-31
  characteristics of, 3-4, 31, 35,
  38-39, 44-45, 49, 94, 110, 170,
  187
    aggression, 105-106
    contempt, 103-104
  definition of, 43-44
  episodes, examples of, 9-10,
  17-18, 19-20, 33-34, 39, 48-
  49, 52-53, 72-73, 85-86, 91,
  94, 97, 100-102, 104-105, 107,
  129-130, 186 (*See also* ODD:
  medication: antidepressant:
  therapeutic effect)
  medication, 59, 71, 107-108
    antidepressant
      antiserotonin uptake

Nancy A. Hagener

About the Author

Nancy A. Hagener, MAEd., is a professional educator of children with learning disabilities. She is a guest speaker for various educational institutions and parent organizations. She is a member of the Council for Exceptional Children and Phi Delta Kappa. Nancy lives with her family in Arizona.

♪

Breinigsville, PA USA
24 August 2010

244204BV00002B/11/A

9 780976 557913